Приятного аппетита

от Ремизов

июнь, 97

THE JEWISH
COOKBOOK

THE JEWISH
COOKBOOK

70 RECIPES CELEBRATING
AN HISTORIC CUISINE

JUDY JACKSON

SMITHMARK

For Rachel, Rebecca, Noah and Sam

© 1996 Anness Publishing Limited

This edition published in 1996
by SMITHMARK Publishers
a division of US Media Holdings Inc.
16 East 32nd Street
New York
NY 10016
USA

SMITHMARK books are available for bulk purchase for sales
and promotion and premium use. For details write or call the
manager of special sales, SMITHMARK Publishers, a division of US Media
Holdings Inc., 16 East 32nd Street, New York, NY 10016; (212 532 6600)

ISBN 0-7651-9916-5

Publisher: Joanna Lorenz
Senior Cookery Editor: Linda Fraser
In-house Editor: Anne Hildyard
Designer: Siân Keogh
Photography: Amanda Heywood, assisted by Vanessa Kellas
Styling: Clare Louise Hunt
Food for Photography: Elizabeth Wolf-Cohen, assisted by Zoe Keen
Illustrator: Madeleine David

Printed in Singapore by Star Standard Industries Pte. Ltd.

ACKNOWLEDGEMENTS
The author would like to thank Stoves plc for their assistance with a gas hob,
Pifco Ltd. and Moulinex Ltd. for supplying slow-cookers which were invaluable
for the recipe testing.

Stoves plc, Stoney Lane, Prestcot, Merseyside L35 2XW

Pifco Ltd. (Russell Hobbs), Failsworth, Manchester M35 OHS

Moulinex Swan Holdings Ltd. Albion Street, Birmingham B1 3DL

CONTENTS

INTRODUCTION

For centuries Jews have moved from country to country, taking their customs and cooking pots with them. The result is that Jewish cuisine, unlike any other, is enormously varied. Observant Jews have always kept to rigid rules, set down in the Bible, about what can and can't be eaten. So wherever they settled they found new foods and adapted them to complement the dishes they already knew.

There arc two distinct Jewish groups – one is *Sephardic* (broadly from the Mediterranean, the Middle and Far East), and the other is *Ashkenazi* (from France, Germany, Russia and Eastern Europe). Sephardic foods include olive oil, peppers and eggplants from Spain, spicy rice from Iraq and Persia and sweet syrupy pastries from Turkey and Greece. Ashkenazi dishes feature carp and goose and desserts such as cheesecake and apple strudel.

What brings the two groups together are the Jewish Festivals and, above all, the celebration of the end of the working week – the Sabbath (*Shabbat*). Whatever the style of mid-week eating, on Friday and Saturday everyone sits down together over long and delicious meals. Jewish people adore eating. They rarely simply go out for a drink. To them a celebration always involves food. When a baby is born there is a party. A child reaching adulthood (13 for a boy, 12 for a girl) has a religious ceremony called a *Barmitzvah* or *Batmitzvah* and this, too, is followed by a party which can take months of

planning. "The Menu" is the main topic of discussion, both before and afterwards. A wedding is even more special and often involves a buffet lunch at the bridegroom's home the day before. A typical Sephardic table would be laden with several platters of meat, rice and stuffed vegetables, followed by nut-filled baklava, date pastries and trays of exotic fruits. Strong black coffee or mint tea would complete the meal.

In English there are no special words associated with offering food to guests. In French you say "Bon Appetit." Translated into Hebrew, this is "Be

Te'avon." Today many people simply say "Enjoy". I hope you will enjoy the dishes I have chosen to represent the mosaic of Jewish cooking.

THE JEWISH KITCHEN

Most people know that Jews don't eat pork. The dietary laws (called *Kashrut*, from which the word 'kosher' comes) explain exactly what is permitted. Camels and hares and any part of an "unclean" animal are not allowed – cows and sheep are allowed. Shellfish and snails are prohibited, while fish with fins and scales can be eaten. Domestic birds like chickens and geese are fine, but birds of prey are not. At the end of a long description in Deuteronomy comes a passage condemning "boiling a kid in its mother's milk." From this comes the idea of not eating any milk or dairy product with meat. So, for anyone unfamiliar with the rules, here is an explanation of what to expect.

INGREDIENTS THAT NEED CARE

MEAT
Pork, ham, and bacon are strictly forbidden and so is any meat from an animal that has not been killed humanely. So meat and poultry must have a "kosher" label. In most countries only the forequarter of an animal is used so rump steak or leg of lamb are not usually available. Products

Choosing the perfect ingredient at a bustling street market in the Mea She'arim district of west Jerusalem.

containing even small amounts of meat stock, gelatin or lard are not allowed.

DAIRY FOOD

Any dairy product like milk, cream or yogurt is never served at the same time, or even just after, a meat meal. So there are no cream sauces with chicken or marinades of lamb in yogurt. After-dinner coffee is served black. After a meat course, cheese is never served.

FISH

Cod, haddock, herring, mackerel, salmon, and sea bass are some of the many fish that are eaten. Monkfish, shrimp, lobster, eels and octopus are among those which are not. Dairy products can certainly be used with fish and eaten after a meal containing fish.

EGGS

Eggs are neutral and can be served with either meat, fish or dairy products. It is the custom to break each egg into a cup before stirring it into a mixture, to avoid possible blood spots – a sensible precaution too, in case the egg is bad.

STOCKS

Homemade stocks can be made from meat, fish or vegetables but chicken or beef stock would never be added to a soup which would later include milk or cream. Kosher meat cubes are available and there is an excellent product to enhance vegetable soups called "Pareve (not real) Chicken Stock Powder."

HIDDEN INGREDIENTS

The accurate labeling of ingredients has encouraged many people to find out more about what they are eating from a health point of view.

Animal fat and gelatin are among the ingredients that observant Jews would avoid, so if you are catering for Jewish friends, it is better to provide totally vegetarian products for them, unless you are buying food from a completely kosher shop.

Great care is taken in selecting the most perfect specimens of etrog (*a type of citrus fruit*), *which is one of the items connected with the festival of Sukkot. This open-air market in Jerusalem is specially set up to sell the necessary traditional items used for this festival. The other plants used are* aravot (*willow*), haddasim (*myrtles*) *and* lulav (*palm branch*). *Sukkot is one of the most colorful and happy festivals in the Jewish calendar.*

INGREDIENTS

BAGELS

A bagel is a traditional ring-shaped Jewish bread with a golden, shiny crust. Bagels have a dense, chewy texture due to the way they are cooked, which involves boiling them first, then baking. Bagels come plain or with a variety of toppings, including sesame seeds, poppy seeds, onion and garlic. A typical delicatessen snack is bagels filled with cream cheese and smoked salmon, known as lox.

BARLEY

Traditionally eaten as a filling, satisfying food in eastern Europe, barley is now added to slow-cooked meat dishes and soups for its delicious, nutty flavor and slightly chewy texture.

BULGUR

This consists of wheat grains which have been partially cooked, dried and crushed to make a grain that is quick to cook. It is used in tabbouleh, a wheat-based salad, and pilafs.

CHALLAH

This classic Jewish yeast bread is made with eggs and has a light, airy texture. It is served on the Sabbath, and at holiday and everyday meals. It can be

A selection of shelled, unshelled and ground nuts, pomegranate and dates.

made in any size or shape, and often comes in the form of a braided loaf.

DATES

A brown, slightly wrinkled fruit with a very sweet flesh. Dates have been eaten since biblical times and they are still commonly used today in pastries, breads and sweetmeats.

FLAT NOODLES

Usually made with egg, in addition to flour and water, noodles feature as an accompaniment to many Jewish dishes.

HONEY

Honey has long been used as a sweetener, and in Jewish cooking it is used to make a traditional honey cake for Rosh Hashanah, to make sure the new year will be sweet.

LENTILS

Red lentils disintegrate during cooking and so are useful thickeners for soup, while the flat grey-green ones retain their texture and color.

MATZO

A thin, crisp unleavened bread, made from flour and water, which comes in crackers in various shapes and sizes, it is

traditionally eaten during the Passover holiday and can also be used to make sweet or savoury dumplings.

MATZO MEAL

This is available in different textures; medium and fine. It is used for coating foods to be fried, and for dumplings added to chicken soup. The finest texture is used in Passover cakes.

NUTS

Nuts are widely used in Jewish cuisine. Salted pistachios are often eaten as a nibble before dinner, while chestnuts are added to dishes such as vegetarian cholent and stuffings. Hazelnuts are ground and used instead of flour for desserts and sponge cakes, and pecan nuts are used to decorate brownies. The small creamy colored pine nut is often toasted and sprinkled over lamb or added to pilafs. Available whole, flaked or ground, almonds are used in a wide variety of dishes: in desserts, biscuits, flans and included in stuffings for poultry.

PITA BREAD

This is a flatbread made with white or brown flour. When warmed, it puffs up and can be split to form a pocket to stuff with falafel, hummus or salad.

Clockwise from top left: pita bread, matzo, matzo crackers, challah, matzo and bagels.

Clockwise from top left: smatana, tahini, rose water and honey.

Clockwise from top left: lentils, flat noodles, barley, vermicelli, matzo meal and bulgur.

POMEGRANATE

A large fruit with a leathery red skin, containing hundreds of small seeds, each surrounded by brilliant red, juicy flesh. The seeds are separated by a yellow bitter membrane, which is inedible. In Jewish cooking, the pomegranate is squeezed like a lemon for its tart-sweet juice. The juice is used as a marinade for meat, to add flavor and color.

ROSE WATER

The distilled essence of rose petals is used to perfume desserts and pastries such as baklava.

SOUR CREAM

Sour cream is widely used in sauces for both sweet or savory dishes.

TAHINI

This is a thick, oily paste ground of toasted sesame seeds that adds a distinctive nutty flavor to hummus. The oil separates out but is easily beaten back into a paste.

VERMICELLI

Vermicelli is very fine strands of pasta. Known in Jewish cuisine as *lockshen*, it is often added to chicken soup.

THE JEWISH KITCHEN

SHABBAT – THE SABBATH

Work is not allowed on sabbaths or festivals. Since cooking is considered work – however enjoyable – everything has to be prepared beforehand. So inventive cooks have devised recipes that can be made before Friday evening or left to cook slowly overnight for lunch the next day. For both meals the table is set with a fine white cloth and the best china and glass. There is always wine and braided white loaves called *challah*.

Long ago, the centerpiece would be a large stuffed fish (the original gefilte fish), but in hard times when people could no longer afford the whole fish they just used the stuffing and formed it into small balls. These modern gefilte fish balls are often served to begin the meal. Whereas they used to be made by laborious chopping, now they are made much more easily with a food processor.

The best known shabbat dish is called *cholent*. It is a large casserole full of meat, vegetables and any combination of beans, barley, chickpeas or potatoes. A non-stick frying pan is good for browning the meat first and a slow cooker – or crockpot – will produce a meltingly tender result. Designed for overnight cooking, it is a perfect all-in-one dish for working people.

EVERYDAY COOKING

Because of the strict separation between milk and meat, observant Jews keep separate utensils, so it is not uncommon to find two complete sets of crockery, saucepans and cutlery in the kitchen.

To compensate for the outlay in kitchen tools, traditional Jewish food is often based on inexpensive fresh ingredients, like fish, vegetables and chicken. Kosher processed and packaged meals are available but they are rarely as good as home-made. The essential ingredients of the dishes I have chosen are time and a love of cooking.

Festival Foods

The foods eaten on each festival sometimes date back to biblical times. The cycle begins in September/October.

Here is a selection of some of the most appropriate dishes to serve at each festival.

Rosh Hashanah – New Year

Jewish New Year is not about staying up till midnight and drinking champagne! It is a happy yet serious festival when sugar or honey are included so that the coming year should be sweet.

Special sweet dishes include:
Turkey breasts with wine and grapes
Apple-stuffed duck
Honey cake
Baklava

Yom Kippur – The Day Of Atonement

This is a 24-hour fast when no food or drink (even water) is allowed. Naturally great thought goes into what is eaten before and afterwards!

Filling dishes include:
Chicken soup with lockshen
Lamb with lentils and apricots
Fried fish
Home-made pickled cucumbers
Potato salad

A typical Passover celebration, with symbolic foods telling their story of the oppression of the Jews and their flight from Egypt.

Tabernacles – Sukkot

For one week in autumn, temporary huts (called *Sukkot*) are used for eating and even sleeping. It's a reminder of the travels and unstable life of the ancient Israelites in the desert.

Warming meals include:
Barley soup
Golden chicken
Stuffed vegetables
Pear and almond flan with
   chocolate sauce

Hanukkah – The Festival Of Lights

This winter festival is a treat for children, with eight days of candle lighting and little presents.

Special fried dishes include:
Falafel with hummus
Potato Latkes
Veal schnitzels with lemon
Pancakes

Purim

During this festival a long story is told about the downfall of a wicked enemy, Haman. This is followed by drinks, a great meal and taking small gifts of food to neighbors.

Presents to take include:
Ma-amoul – date pastries
Flaked almond cookies
Haman's Ears
Chocolate apricots

Passover

The celebration of Passover dates back to biblical times. The Jews escaped from the tyrannical persecution of the Pharoah in Egypt and left in such haste that their bread dough had no time to rise. The story is retold every year at a special meal called the *Seder* (which incidentally was being celebrated at the Last Supper). The spring festival lasts

The haggadah – *the book which tells the Exodus story – with wine and matzo.*

for eight days. Nothing leavened is eaten and Jewish homes are even cleared of all traces of bread, flour, biscuits and cereals. Matzo (or *matzah*) which is unleavened bread is eaten instead of bread. The thin crispy squares (or smaller crackers) are sold in packets. Ground matzo meal is used instead of flour.

Cooking for the week is a challenge, but there are such delights as featherweight nut cakes and light-as-air dumplings for soup, called *Luft Knaidlach*. To be successful in making some of these dishes, two vital pieces of equipment are required – an electric mixer and blender or a food processor.

Specialities for Passover include:
Haroset – an apple and nut mixture
Luft knaidlach and matzo *kleis*
   dumplings
Roasted lamb with zucchini
Chicken breasts with burnt almond
   stuffing
Coconut pyramids
Cinnamon balls
Jerusalem artichoke soup
Halibut in lemon sauce
Matzo pancakes
Hazelnut sponge with vanilla sauce

Seven weeks later in early summer comes the reminder of Moses receiving the Tablets of the Law on Mount Sinai when it's a tradition to eat dairy foods.

Suitable dishes include:
Fresh beets with sour cream
Smoked salmon rolls
Tomato and red pepper soup
Cucumber and fish salad
Cheesecake

SHABBAT – THE SABBATH
Every Saturday is a day of rest, relaxation and no cooking. The enjoyment comes from eating all the dishes which have been prepared one or two days in advance.

Specially good ones include:
Chopped liver with egg and onion
Challah – braided white bread
Braised beef with vegetables
Beef cholent with hamin eggs

Special pancakes for Passover, shown here with a delicious savory topping.

Slow cooked lamb with barley
Vegetarian cholent
Spicy carrots
Sliced eggplant with garlic and
    tomato glaze
Red fruit salad
Fruit coulis
Peach kuchen
Cinnamon rolls

APPETIZERS AND SOUPS

The serious business of eating starts before dinner with bowls of olives, almonds or pistachio nuts. Some people even crunch whole chili peppers! Weekday or special meals often begin with soup. Since the story of Esau and Jacob, who quarrelled over a bowl of "red pottage", soup has always been popular. Everyone knows the legendary value of Chicken Soup. Called "Jewish penicillin" it is a magical broth that cures all ills and brings comfort and warmth.

Soups in Eastern Europe had to be thick and filling in winter, so they often contained lentils, beans or barley. One version called Krupnik used dried mushrooms for flavor when meat was scarce. Nowadays the fashionable dried mushrooms would be more expensive than the meat!

Chopped Liver with Egg and Onion

Traditionally, chicken fat was used and the mixture chopped by hand. This modern recipe calls for chicken stock and a blender.

INGREDIENTS

Serves 4

For the liver pâté
8 ounces chicken livers
3 tablespoons oil
1 onion, chopped
3 tablespoons chicken stock

For the egg and onion
2–3 eggs, hard-cooked and shelled
2–3 scallions, chopped
2 tablespoons chicken stock
salt and ground black pepper
olives and gherkins, to serve
scallion strips, to garnish

1 Preheat the broiler. Place the chicken livers on an oiled wire rack in a broiler pan and cook under the broiler for 2–3 minutes on each side.

2 Heat the oil in a frying pan and sauté the onion until golden. Add the livers and cook briefly, breaking them up with a fork so that they are no longer pink inside. Season.

3 Add the chicken stock, turn down the heat and continue cooking the liver and onions for a few minutes. Spoon them into a blender or food processor and process until a smooth paste is formed.

4 To make the egg and onion mixture, put the eggs with the scallion in the bowl of a blender or food processor. There's no need to wash it first, as it does no harm to flavor the eggs with a little bit of chopped liver. Add the stock, season and blend until smooth.

5 Serve the chopped liver in a small mound with some of the egg and onion on the side. Serve with olives and gherkins and garnished with the scallion strips.

Eggplant Dip

An appetizer to serve with drinks and crisp sticks of raw vegetables. Eggplant is very popular and is almost a staple food in Israel.

INGREDIENTS

Serves 4 as an appetizer – more as a dip
2 eggplants (about 10 ounces each)
2 onions, chopped
²/₃ cup olive oil
3 garlic cloves, crushed
juice of 1 lemon
salt and ground black pepper
sprigs of cilantro, to garnish
black and green olives, to serve

1 Preheat the broiler. Cut the eggplants in half lengthwise and put them on a sheet of foil, skin side up. Broil at least 2 inches from the heat for 20 minutes. The skin will start to wrinkle and the flesh will become slightly smoky and soft.

2 Meanwhile, sauté the onions in a frying pan over a medium heat in about 4 tablespoons oil, add the garlic and cook until they are soft but not brown. Season.

3 Scoop the flesh out of the eggplant halves and put it into a blender with the onion and garlic. Add the lemon juice.

4 With the blades running, slowly pour in the remaining olive oil to make a very smooth mixture. Taste again for seasoning.

5 Spoon the dip into bowls. Garnish with sprigs of cilantro and serve with black and green olives.

Falafel

A typical street food in Israel, hot, crisp falafel are served in warm pita bread.

INGREDIENTS

Serves 4 – makes about 18 small balls

1¼ cups dried chickpeas
3 garlic cloves
1 teaspoon cumin seeds
1 teaspoon coriander seeds
a handful of cilantro,
   finely chopped
a handful of flat leaf parsley,
   finely chopped
¼ teaspoon chili powder
1 tablespoon lemon juice
1 teaspoon salt
1 teaspoon baking powder
oil, for deep frying
ground black pepper
pita bread and hummus, to serve

1 Soak the chickpeas in water overnight. Drain and discard the water.

2 Crush the garlic and grind the cumin and coriander seeds with a mortar and pestle. Put the chickpeas in a food processor and process until they are broken up. Add the garlic, spices, fresh herbs, salt and the chili powder. Process in a blender until smooth.

3 Add lemon juice, taste for seasoning and add ground black pepper or more spice to taste. Let stand for about 30 minutes.

4 Stir in the baking powder and form the mixture into small balls. Fry in hot oil for a couple of minutes or until the falafel are golden. Drain and serve with pita bread and hummus.

Hummus

Traditionally served with falafel, this chickpea and sesame seed dip is also good with crackers or raw vegetables. The tahini – sesame seed paste – is available from Jewish or Arabic delicatessens. It's worth making twice the quantity as hummus freezes well.

INGREDIENTS

Serves 4 as an appetizer – more as a dip

1¼ cups chickpeas,
   soaked overnight
½ cup tahini paste
2 garlic cloves, crushed
juice of 1–2 lemons
4 tablespoons olive oil
salt
cayenne pepper and flat leaf parsley,
   to garnish

1 Drain the chickpeas and cook in fresh boiling water for 10 minutes. Reduce the heat and simmer for about an hour or until soft. Drain the chickpeas, reserving the cooking liquid.

COOK'S TIP

If using a can (14 ounces) of chickpeas, omit the soaking and boiling and follow the instructions from Step 2.

2 Put the chickpeas, tahini paste, garlic and a little lemon juice into a food processor. Process until smooth. Season, add enough cooking liquid to process to a creamy consistency. More lemon juice or liquid can be added as the hummus gets stiffer after resting.

3 Spoon the hummus onto plates, swirl it with a knife and drizzle with olive oil. Sprinkle with cayenne pepper and garnish with parsley.

Mushroom Pâté

A vegetarian alternative to chopped liver. Frying the onion in butter gives a rich flavor, but you can use oil instead.

INGREDIENTS

Serves 4

2 tablespoons olive oil or butter
2 onions, chopped
4½ cups mushrooms, chopped or coarsely sliced
1 cup ground almonds
handful of parsley, stalks removed
salt and ground black pepper
flat leaf parsley, for garnish
thin slices of toast, and cucumber, endive and celery sticks, to serve

1 Heat the olive oil or butter in a frying pan and sauté the onions over moderate heat until golden. Keep stirring the onions as you fry them. Take care not to burn the butter, as it takes a few minutes for the onions to turn opaque and then start to brown.

2 Add the mushrooms and continue frying until the juices start to run. Season well.

3 Put the fried onion and mushrooms into a blender or food processor with the juices. Add the ground almonds and parsley and process briefly. The pâté can either be smooth or left slightly chunky. Taste again for seasoning.

4 Spoon the pâté into individual pots. Garnish with flat leaf parsley and serve with thin slices of toast and sticks of cucumber, endive and celery.

Barley Soup

Eastern Europe has winters that are bitterly cold and traditional soups often contained beans, lentils and barley. In a climate with less fierce winters, a lighter soup with only one "filler" is more appealing, but the base of a good stock makes all the difference to the flavor.

INGREDIENTS

Serves 4

2 pounds meaty bones (lamb, beef or veal)
3³/₄ cups water
3 carrots
4 celery stalks
1 onion
2 tablespoons oil
2 tablespoons barley
salt and ground black pepper

COOK'S TIP

All soups taste better with homemade stock. The long slow simmering can be done well in advance and stocks freeze well. A quick (and more salty) version can be made using water and a stock cube, but it won't have the same flavor.

1 Preheat the oven to 400°F. To prepare the meat stock, brown the lamb, beef or veal bones in a roasting pan in the oven for about 30 minutes. Remove the bones and put them in a large saucepan, cover with water and bring to a boil.

2 Use a metal spoon to skim off the froth which comes to the surface and then cover the pan and simmer for at least 2 hours. Chop the carrots, celery and onion finely. Heat the oil in a saucepan and sauté the vegetables in the oil for about 1 minute. Strain the stock into the pan.

3 Add the barley to the pan of vegetables and continue cooking for about 1 hour, until the barley is soft. Season the soup with plenty of salt and pepper, transfer to serving bowls and serve hot.

Chicken Soup with Lockshen

The best of all soup recipes, it is simple to make if you follow two rules: make it the day before and try to find a boiling fowl which has much more flavor than a roasting bird.

INGREDIENTS

Serves 6–8

6½ pounds boiling chicken, including the giblets but not the liver
8 cups cold water
2 onions, halved
2 carrots
5 stalks celery
a handful of fine vermicelli (*lockshen*), about 4 ounces
salt and ground black pepper
fresh bread, to serve (optional)

1 Put the washed chicken into a very large pan with the giblets. Add the water and bring to a boil over high heat. Skim off the white froth that comes to the top and then add the halved onions, carrots and stalks of celery. Season with ground black pepper only.

2 When the liquid comes to a boil again, turn the heat to low, cover and simmer the chicken and the stock for at least 2 hours. Keep an eye on the water level and add a little more so that the chicken is always covered.

3 When the chicken is tender, remove it from the pan, take the meat off the bones, and reserve it for another use. Put the bones back in the soup and continue cooking for another 1 hour. There should be at least 4 cups of soup.

4 Strain the soup into a large bowl and chill overnight. When it is totally chilled it may form a jelly and a pale layer of fat will have settled on the top. Remove the fat with a spoon and discard.

5 Bring the soup to a boil again, season to taste and add the vermicelli (*lockshen*). Boil for about 8 minutes and serve in large bowls, with fresh bread, if using.

White Bean Soup

Use either navy beans or lima beans for this velvety soup. As with all meat-based soups, real butter or cream is not included.

INGREDIENTS

Serves 4

³/₄ cup dried white beans or 14 ounce
   can cannellini or lima beans
2 large onions, chopped
4 celery stalks, chopped
1 parsnip, chopped
2–3 tablespoons oil
4 cups meat stock
salt and ground black pepper
chopped cilantro and paprika,
   to garnish
fresh bread, to serve

1 If using dried beans, soak them overnight in cold water. Drain and boil rapidly in fresh water for 10 minutes, drain and simmer in fresh water until soft. Reserve the liquid and discard any bean skins on the surface.

2 Heat the oil and sauté the onions, celery and parsnip for 3 minutes.

3 Add the cooked beans (if using canned ones, drain them first and discard the liquid). Add the meat stock and continue cooking until the vegetables are tender. Allow the soup to cool slightly and using a food processor or hand blender, blend the soup until it is velvety smooth.

4 Reheat the soup gently, adding some of the bean liquid or some more water if it is too thick. Adjust the seasoning to taste.

5 To serve, transfer the soup into wide bowls. Garnish with cilantro, sprinkle with a little paprika and serve with fresh bread.

Chicken Soup with Luft Knaidlach

During the festival of Passover when no bread or pasta is eaten, chicken soup is served with light dumplings (*knaidlach*). There are two kinds, both of Ashkenazi (Eastern European) origin. The secret of making them light is to make both mixtures soft, and to chill the mixture before cooking.

INGREDIENTS

Makes enough for 8, allowing 3 small balls per person

¾ cup matzo meal
⅔ cup cold water
1 teaspoon salt
pinch ground ginger
3 eggs, well-beaten
6 tablespoons oil
1 quantity Chicken Soup

1 Mix the matzo meal with the water, salt and ginger. Add the eggs and oil and chill the mixture in the fridge for a few hours.

2 Form the mixture into small ¾-inch diameter balls, wetting your hands or dipping them in a little more meal as you work to prevent the mixture from sticking. Don't add too much meal or it will make the dumplings heavy.

3 Bring a large pan of water to a boil and gently put in the *knaidlach*. As the water comes to a boil again, they will rise to the surface and double in size. Cook in gently boiling water for 20 minutes.

4 Meanwhile reheat the Chicken Soup. Drain the *knaidlach*, pouring away the cooking water and float the dumplings in the soup. Transfer to soup bowls and serve.

Chicken Soup with Matzo Kleis Balls

INGREDIENTS

Serves 6–8

2 matzo (sheets of unleavened bread)
1 onion, chopped
2 tablespoons oil
handful of parsley
2 eggs
2–4 tablespoons medium-ground matzo meal
pinch of ground ginger
1 quantity Chicken Soup
salt and ground black pepper

> —— COOK'S TIP ——
>
> You can make both types of dumpling well in advance, but the balls should be kept chilled. They freeze well, so you can cook half and freeze half. To cook from frozen, defrost for about 1 hour before cooking.

1 Soak the matzo in cold water for about 5 minutes and then drain and squeeze them dry.

2 Fry the onion in the oil until golden. Chop the parsley, reserving a few sprigs for the garnish. Whisk the eggs slightly.

3 Mix together the soaked matzo, fried onion, parsley and eggs. Season with salt, pepper and ginger and add about 1 tablespoon of matzo meal. Chill for at least 1 hour.

4 Roll the mixture into small balls, drop them into the fast-boiling soup and cook for about 20 minutes. Serve, garnished with the parsley.

Jerusalem Artichoke Soup

INGREDIENTS

Serves 4

2–4 tablespoons butter
2 cups sliced mushrooms
2 onions, chopped
1 pound Jerusalem artichokes, peeled
    and sliced
1¼ cups vegetable stock
1¼ cups milk
salt and ground black pepper

COOK'S TIP

To make a light vegetable stock, simply boil some carrots, onion, leeks or root vegetables in a large pan of water. Simmer for about 30 minutes and then strain.

1 Melt the butter in a saucepan and sauté the mushrooms for 1 minute. Put them on a plate and then sauté the onions and artichokes, adding a little more butter if necessary. Keep on stirring the vegetables, without allowing them to brown.

2 Add the vegetable stock to the pan and bring to a boil. Simmer until the artichokes are soft and then season according to taste.

3 Purée the soup with a hand blender or food processor, adding the milk slowly until smooth. Reheat the soup, return the mushrooms to the pan and serve.

Tomato and Red Pepper Soup

A late summer soup using very ripe peppers and tomatoes. It can be served cold, but won't be nearly as tasty if made with imported winter vegetables which have a less vibrant flavor.

INGREDIENTS

Serves 4

5 large tomatoes
2–4 tablespoons olive oil
1 onion, chopped
1 pound thinly sliced red or
    orange bell peppers
2 tablespoons tomato paste
a pinch of sugar
2 cups vegetable stock
4 tablespoons sour cream (optional)
salt and ground black pepper
chopped fresh dill, to garnish

1 Skin the tomatoes by plunging them into boiling water for 30 seconds. Chop the flesh and reserve any juice.

2 Heat half the oil in a saucepan and sauté the onion over moderate heat until soft. Add the peppers and the remaining oil and continue cooking, without browning the vegetables, until they start to soften.

3 Stir in the chopped tomatoes, tomato paste, the seasoning, sugar and a few tablespoons of stock and simmer until the vegetables are tender.

4 Stir in the rest of the stock and blend until smooth. Strain to remove the skins, and season.

5 Pour into bowls, swirl in the cream, if using, and garnish with dill.

FISH AND VEGETARIAN DISHES

Concern about animal welfare means that many Jewish people prefer not to eat meat, so fish is very popular. Although smoked salmon is a must for special occasions like weddings and barmitzvahs, it's just as usual to serve both herring and fried gefilte fish, which are cheap. When entertaining friends, it is often easier to choose a dinner based on vegetables and fish. I've included some old favorites as well as several new inventions. The vegetarian cholent for Saturday lunch is a warming winter dish which would be equally good for busy working cooks, as it simmers all day and needs no attention.

Halibut in Lemon Sauce

INGREDIENTS

Serves 4

1 small onion
1 large carrot
1¼ cups water
½ teaspoon sugar
4 halibut steaks, about 6 ounces each
2 lemons
3 egg yolks
salt and ground black pepper
asparagus and boiled potatoes, to serve

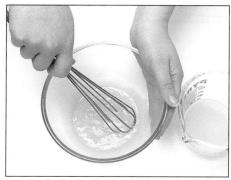

1 Slice the onion and carrot and bring to a boil with the water in a wide pan. Season with sugar, salt and pepper and simmer for 15 minutes. Remove the vegetable pieces with a slotted spoon and set aside. Lower the halibut steaks into the cooking liquid and cook over low heat for about 8 minutes.

2 You can tell when the halibut steaks are cooked by inserting a knife near the bone: if the fish looks opaque it is cooked. Lift the steaks out and arrange them on a shallow dish. Cover with a sheet of foil if you want to serve them hot. Bring the cooking liquid to a boil again and reduce it over high heat for a few minutes.

3 Meanwhile, to make the lemon sauce, cut a few slices from the top of each lemon and set them aside for garnishing. Squeeze the juice from the remaining pieces of lemon, whisk the egg yolks in a bowl and stir in the lemon juice.

4 Strain the reduced cooking liquid onto the egg and lemon mixture and pour it back into the pan. Stir the sauce over very low heat, taking great care not to let it boil. When it thickens, pour it over the fish. Serve the fish hot or cold, with asparagus and boiled potatoes.

Whole Cooked Salmon

Farmed salmon has made this fish more affordable and less of a treat, but a whole salmon still features as a centerpiece at parties. It is never served with cold meats but is accompanied by salads and mayonnaise. As with all fish, the taste depends on freshness, and on not overcooking it, so although you need to start early, the cooking time is short.

INGREDIENTS

Serves about 10 as part of a buffet
5–6 pounds fresh whole salmon
2 tablespoons oil
1 lemon
salt and ground black pepper
lemon wedges, cucumber and fresh dill
   sprigs, to garnish

1 Preheat the oven to 400°F. Wash the salmon and dry it well, inside and out. Pour half the oil onto a large piece of heavy foil and place the fish in the center.

2 Put a few slices of lemon inside the salmon and arrange some more on the top. Season well and sprinkle over the remaining oil. Wrap up the foil to make a loose package. Put the package on another sheet of foil or a baking sheet and cook in the oven for 10 minutes. Turn off the oven, don't open the door and leave for several hours. As it cools, the salmon cooks but stays moist.

3 To serve the same day, remove the foil and peel off the skin. If you are keeping it for the following day, leave the skin on and chill the fish overnight. Arrange the fish on a large platter and garnish with lemon wedges, cucumber cut into thin ribbons and sprigs of dill.

Smoked Salmon Rolls

Smoked salmon is a favorite filling for snacks and sandwiches.

INGREDIENTS

Makes about 20 small appetizers
12 ounces best quality smoked salmon
2 lemons
bunch of fresh dill, to garnish

Fish filling
8 ounces smoked mackerel fillet
3 tablespoons sour cream
ground black pepper

Cheese and herb filling
bunch of mixed herbs: chives and
    parsley and chervil
8 ounces cottage or ricotta cheese
salt and ground black pepper

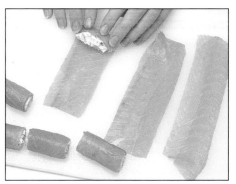

1 To make the fish filling, remove the skin from the mackerel and make sure there are no bones. Blend or mash the fish with the sour cream. Add pepper but no salt, as both the salmon and mackerel are quite salty. To make the cheese filling, simply chop the herbs and stir them into the soft cheese and season well.

2 Cut the smoked salmon into strips about 1 x 3 inches. Put a teaspoon of the chosen filling at one end and roll up, smoothing the sides with a knife to make sure the filling is neatly enclosed.

3 Arrange the rolls on a platter and garnish with lemon and dill.

Cucumber and Fish Salad

A cool dish for summer – ideal served on individual plates for lunch or on a large platter as part of a buffet. Instead of cod you can use haddock fillet or, for a more special occasion, sea bass.

INGREDIENTS

Serves 4–8
2 large cucumbers
1¼ pounds fresh cod fillet, skinned
1 scallion, chopped
small bunch of fresh dill
5 tablespoons milk
4 tablespoons mayonnaise
2 tablespoons sour cream or
    plain yogurt
³/₄ cup cooked fava beans or peas
    (optional)
4 black or green olives and cucumber
    ribbons, to garnish
salt

1 Peel one of the cucumbers and cut the flesh into dice. With a vegetable peeler, remove about six long thin strips from the other cucumber and then cut the rest into dice as well. Sprinkle the pieces with salt and let drain on absorbent paper towels.

2 Put the fish in a pan with the scallion, a few sprigs of dill and the milk. Season well and poach gently for a few minutes until the fish begins to flake. Lift it out with a slotted spoon and set aside to cool.

3 Wash and drain the cucumber and dry well. Mix the mayonnaise with the sour cream or yogurt, stir in the cucumber, fava beans or peas, if using, and finally fold in the fish.

4 Spoon the mixture onto individual plates, and garnish with olives and cucumber ribbons.

Gefilte Fish

There are two ways of cooking this popular snack, either by poaching or frying.

INGREDIENTS

Makes about 24 small balls

2 pounds mixed filleted fish, such as
   carp, porgy, haddock and cod
1 large onion
2 eggs
1–2 teaspoons sugar
10 tablespoons matzo meal
salt and ground black pepper
oil, for frying
flat leaf parsley, to garnish
bottled beet and horseradish sauce,
   to serve

1 Cut the fish and the onion into small pieces and process briefly together in a food processor. Add the eggs, sugar, salt and pepper and continue to blend until the mixture is smooth. Taste the mixture (raw fresh fish is not unpleasant) and add more seasoning if necessary.

2 Stir in a few spoonfuls of matzo meal and form the mixture into 1-inch balls. The mixture will seem quite soft.

3 Roll the balls in the remaining matzo meal and chill in the fridge until you are ready to fry them. Heat a large pan of oil until it reaches a temperature of 375°F. Fry the balls for about 4–5 minutes, until they are crisp and golden brown.

4 Lift them out with a slotted spoon and drain very well. Cool.

5 Serve cold, with beet and horseradish sauce, garnished with flat leaf parsley.

Fried Fish

Fried fish is nearly always served cold. If you have never tried it, you are missing a real speciality. A tray of assorted fish is usual, but you can use one variety if you prefer. The usual accompaniment is potato salad and pickled cucumbers.

INGREDIENTS

Serves 8

2 sand dab, about 8 ounces each
2 flounder, about 1 pound each
1 thick cod fillet, about
    1 pound, skinned
6¼ cups oil, for frying
3 tablespoons flour
8–10 tablespoons matzo meal
4 eggs
salt and ground black pepper
lemon wedges, to garnish
potato salad and pickled cucumbers,
    to serve

1 Wash and dry the fish very well. Leave the sand dab whole, but cut the flounder across the main bone in the center into three sections. Cut the cod fillet into two or three pieces. Start heating the oil in a large deep pan. It will take 4–6 minutes for 1 inch of oil to reach the right temperature (375°F). If you haven't got a thermometer, then drop a cube of bread into the oil and it should brown in 30 seconds.

2 Put the flour and the matzo meal on separate plates and the eggs in a glass dish. Season the eggs and the matzo meal.

3 Dip each piece of fish first into the flour and then into the beaten egg. Lift it out immediately and dip it into the matzo meal.

4 Lower the fish into the hot oil. Don't put in too many pieces as this reduces the temperature of the oil. Fry for about 6 minutes. Turn the fish over, and when it is crisp and brown, lift it out with a slotted spoon. Drain over the pan and cool on paper towels. Serve with potato salad and pickled cucumbers, garnished with lemon.

Stuffed Vegetables

Cabbage or grape leaves are often used for stuffing. You can use any vegetable, such as onions or tomatoes. Bell peppers and zucchini are also good eaten cold.

INGREDIENTS

Serves 6–8
2 small red and 2 small yellow bell peppers
4 zucchini
2–4 tablespoons olive oil
1 cup basmati rice
2 dried peaches or apricots
1/4 teaspoon tomato paste
pinch ground cinnamon
1/4 teaspoon paprika
small bunch flat leaf parsley
salt and ground black pepper

1 Preheat the oven to 375°F. Cut the tops off the peppers and remove the seeds and membranes.

2 Cut the ends off the zucchini and remove the centers with a corer.

3 Heat half the oil in a roasting pan for 5 minutes. Put in the vegetables and roast for about 20 minutes. Drizzle the remaining oil over the top.

4 Meanwhile, cook the rice. Bring a large pan of water to a boil, add the rice and boil for about 8 minutes or until tender, but not mushy. Drain.

5 Snip the dried peaches or apricots into slivers with kitchen scissors, and stir into the rice with the tomato paste, spices and seasoning. Chop some of the parsley and mix about 3 tablespoons into the rice. Pour a little oil from the vegetables into the rice.

6 Cool the vegetables slightly and stuff with the rice. Put the tops on the peppers and arrange the vegetables on a serving dish. Garnish with parsley.

Vegetarian Cholent

The slow-cooked meal for sabbath lunch is called *cholent*. It is usually a meat dish but here is a vegetarian version. The intense flavor comes from slow simmering of the vegetables.

INGREDIENTS

Serves 6
6 onions
3 carrots
4 potatoes
6 stalks celery
3–5 tablespoons oil
10 ounces Portobello mushrooms
1 tablespoon paprika
4 tablespoons soy sauce
1/2 cup barley
2 cups boiling water
salt and ground black pepper

1 Cut the onions into quarters and the carrots and potatoes into 3/4-inch dice. Cut the celery and stalks into 1-inch pieces.

2 Heat half of the oil in a large frying pan and sauté the onions until they begin to turn brown. Add the carrots and cook for about 1 minute. Transfer the onions, carrots and celery to the slow cooker or crockpot.

3 Sauté the mushrooms in the remaining oil and add them to the cooker. Sprinkle the paprika over the oil and cook briefly. Add the soy sauce, the barley and the boiling water and stir.

4 Put the potatoes in the pot with the liquid, season well and cover. Cook on the lowest heat for at least 6 hours or, for the authentic version, leave to cook overnight.

Eggplants with Cheese

Cheese is never served as part of meat dishes. However, it often features as part of a fish or vegetarian buffet.

INGREDIENTS

Serves 4
2 large eggplants
1 pound tomatoes
1 onion
5–7 tablespoons olive oil
6 ounces kosher Dutch or Cheddar
  cheese, thinly sliced
salt and ground black pepper
green salad, to serve

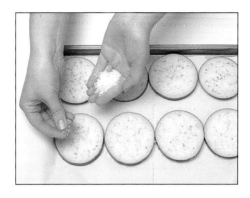

1 Cut the eggplants crosswise into ½-inch slices. Sprinkle them with salt and let drain on absorbent paper towels for 30 minutes. Rinse well and then dry. Skin and slice the tomatoes.

2 Chop the onion finely and sauté it in a few tablespoons of olive oil until golden. Set aside on a plate. Heat the remaining oil and fry the eggplant slices on both sides until brown. Season the vegetables lightly.

3 Preheat the oven to 375°F. Put a layer of eggplant slices into an oiled casserole. Sprinkle over some of the onion and then add some tomato slices. Cover with slices of cheese and continue making layers until all the ingredients are used up, finishing with a layer of cheese.

4 Bake for 30–40 minutes, until the cheese is bubbling and brown. Serve with green salad.

Matzo Pancakes

Passover pancakes are made with matzo meal instead of flour. They can have a savory topping or can simply be served with a liberal sprinkling of sugar and ground cinnamon.

INGREDIENTS

Serves 2 – makes 10 2¹/₂ inch pancakes

For the pancakes
1 egg white
1 whole egg
¹/₂ cup water
pinch salt
1¹/₂ ounces matzo meal
2–3 tablespoons oil

For the savory topping
8 ounces fresh spinach
2 ounces kosher Cheddar cheese, grated
salt and ground black pepper

1 To make the topping: wash the spinach very well, drain and cook in a pan with no extra water for about 1 minute. Put it in a strainer, press out the moisture and then chop it. Season well. Stir in half the cheese.

2 For the pancakes, whisk the egg white and the whole egg until thick and then gradually add the water and salt. Sprinkle in the matzo meal and beat until the mixture is smooth.

3 Heat a little of the oil in a small frying pan, and when it is hot, drop some of the mixture in large spoonfuls into the oil. Almost immediately turn them over and press the pancakes down slightly. Cook for another minute on the other side.

4 Repeat until the mixture is used up. While you are cooking the pancakes, heat the broiler. Arrange the pancakes on a baking sheet. Cover each one with a little of the spinach mixture and grate the remaining cheese over the top. Broil for 1–2 minutes to melt the cheese and serve immediately.

MEAT

*Broiled or roasted meat is often served during the
week rather than at weekends and although veal
or venison could be on the menu, it is more likely
to be lamb or beef. A large brisket is used for the
famous salt beef, and this is one of the best dishes
to order in a restaurant. Kebabs of lamb and spicy
sausages are barbecued.*

*Perhaps the most traditional Jewish food is the
overnight sabbath cholent. The word probably
comes from the French chaud-lent meaning warm
and slow, as the meat is first browned and
surrounded with filling vegetables, then cooked
slowly overnight. Originally everyone took their
pot to the local village bakery but nowadays a
crockpot is the answer.*

Steak Salad

In most countries, kosher beef comes from the forequarter, so it lacks the tenderness of fillet and sirloin. Rare-cooked steak with vegetables makes a very tasty main course salad.

INGREDIENTS

Serves 4

1¼ pounds new potatoes
4 ounces young carrots
1 sprig of mint
8 ounces green beans
1 pound rare-broiled steak or cooked roast beef
⅔ cup mayonnaise
salt and ground black pepper
lettuce leaves, 1 sliced yellow bell pepper and 6 black olives, to garnish

1 Cook the potatoes and carrots separately in boiling salted water with a few mint leaves. When they are tender, pour them into a colander to drain. Cook the green beans for a few minutes in boiling salted water or until they are just tender. Drain and set the beans aside to cool.

2 Cut the steak or roast beef into small dice. Mix the vegetables with the mayonnaise and fold in the meat. Season according to taste.

3 Pile the steak salad into the center of a large dish and garnish with lettuce leaves, sliced yellow pepper and black olives.

Veal Schnitzels with Lemon

In Israel, where meat is expensive, they have perfected the art of turkey farming. Thin slices of turkey breast can be used instead of the original Austrian veal schnitzels.

INGREDIENTS

Serves 4

1½ pounds thin slices of veal or turkey
2 tablespoons flour
3 eggs
1 cup matzo meal
oil, for frying
salt and ground black pepper
2 lemons, cut into wedges, to garnish
lettuce leaves, to serve

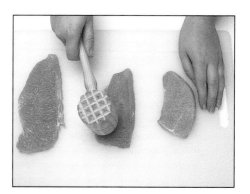

1 Pound the meat with a tenderizing mallet until the slices are very thin. Toss the meat slices in the flour, seasoned with salt and pepper.

2 Beat the eggs in a shallow dish and put the matzo meal on a large plate. Dip the floured veal or turkey first into the beaten eggs, then into the matzo meal, until well coated.

3 Heat about ½ inch oil in a large frying pan and when it is very hot (test with a cube of bread) lower in some of the schnitzels in a single layer. Cook for about 5 minutes and then turn the slices over. Cook the other side for 5 minutes or until golden.

4 Arrange the cooked schnitzels on a serving dish and keep them warm in a low oven until you have finished frying them all. Garnish with wedges of lemon and serve with lettuce leaves.

Peppers Stuffed with Ground Beef

A lunch or buffet dish which makes a change from rice or wheat-stuffed vegetables.

INGREDIENTS

Serves 4
4 red bell peppers
1 onion
2 stalks celery
1 pound lean ground beef
4 tablespoons olive oil
¾ cup button mushrooms
pinch ground cinnamon
salt and ground black pepper
chervil or flat leaf parsley, to garnish
green salad, to serve

1 Cut the tops off the red peppers and reserve them. Remove the seeds and membranes from the peppers. Finely chop the onion and the stalks of celery. Set aside.

2 Sauté the ground beef in a non-stick frying pan for a few minutes, stirring until it is no longer red. Transfer to a plate. Pour half the oil into the frying pan and sauté the chopped vegetables over high heat until the onion starts to brown. Add the mushrooms and stir in the partly cooked beef. Season with the cinnamon, salt and pepper. Cook over low heat for about 30 minutes.

3 Preheat the oven to 375°F. Cut a sliver off the base of each pepper to make sure they stand level, spoon in the beef and vegetable mixture and replace the lids. Arrange in an oiled baking dish, drizzle over the remaining oil and cook in the oven for 30 minutes. Serve with green salad.

---- COOK'S TIP ----

Instead of peppers, you can use large onions or tomatoes. Parboil the onions for about 10 minutes and remove the centers. Carefully scoop out the seeds and flesh of the tomatoes. Fill with the ground beef mixture and bake as above.

Beef Cholent with Beans and Hamin Eggs

There are many different versions of this slow-cooked casserole. This one has the addition of Sephardic whole eggs, which are cooked until they reach a soft texture and are honey-colored.

INGREDIENTS

Serves 6–8

1¼ cups navy, lima or great
   Northern beans
6 small eggs
10 small onions
2 carrots
2–4 tablespoons oil
3–3½ pounds stewing beef, cubed
1 teaspoon paprika
1 teaspoon tomato paste
2½ cups boiling water or beef stock
salt and ground black pepper

1 Soak the beans in cold water overnight. Drain and bring to a boil in fresh water. Cook rapidly for 10 minutes, skimming off the white froth and any bean skins that come to the surface. Drain and reserve the cooking liquid for another use. Hard-cook the eggs for 10 minutes.

2 Preheat a crockpot to Low. Halve the onions and dice the carrots. Heat half the oil in a pan and sauté the onions until golden brown, then transfer to the slow cooker with the carrots and beans. Brown the beef in the remaining oil and place on top of the vegetables. Arrange the eggs between the cubes of beef.

3 Stir the paprika, tomato paste and seasoning into the oil left in the pan and cook for 1 minute. Add the boiling water or stock to deglaze the pan and pour over the meat and eggs.

4 Cover the pot and let the *cholent* cook for at least 8 hours or as long as 20 hours. Take out the eggs, remove the shells and return them to the casserole before serving.

COOK'S TIP

For overnight cooking it is best to use a slow cooker, since the liquid does not evaporate. In a conventional oven, cook the cholent overnight, at 225°F, but add enough water or stock to almost fill the pot so it does not dry out.

Lamb with Lentils and Apricots

INGREDIENTS

Serves 4–6

2 large onions
2 large carrots
2–4 tablespoons oil
2 pounds lean lamb
2 inch cinnamon stick or
　½ teaspoon ground cinnamon
¼ teaspoon ground turmeric
¼ teaspoon cayenne pepper
1 cup green lentils
4 cups water
12 dried apricots
chopped fresh parsley, to garnish

1 Preheat the oven to 350°F. Cut the onions and carrots into large chunks. Heat half the oil in a flameproof casserole and sauté the vegetables until the onion starts to brown. Put the vegetables on a plate and set aside.

2 Cut the lamb into 1-inch cubes and sauté over medium heat, adding more oil if necessary to brown them all over. Add the cinnamon stick or ground cinnamon and sprinkle the rest of the spices over the lamb.

3 Rinse the lentils and add them to the casserole with the vegetables. Stir in 3 cups boiling water, season and bring to a boil. Cover and transfer to the oven.

4 Cook for 1 hour and check to see that the lentils haven't absorbed all the liquid, adding the remaining water if necessary. Cook for another hour.

5 Add the apricots and press them down under the liquid, turn off the oven and leave them to swell for about 20 minutes. Remove the cinnamon stick if using, check the seasoning and stir in a little more water if it seems too dry. Garnish with chopped parsley.

Braised Beef with Vegetables

On Friday evenings in the winter sabbath begins early, at dusk. A rich-tasting braised beef casserole is ideal, as it can be started in the afternoon and left to cook slowly. By dinnertime it will be tender and piping hot.

INGREDIENTS

Serves 6–8

2–3 tablespoons oil
3½ pounds rolled brisket or rolled beef
　rib roast
8 small onions
2 large carrots
1 head celery
2 cups beef stock
salt and ground black pepper
sprig of flat leaf parsley, to garnish

1 Preheat the oven to 350°F. Heat the oil in a casserole and brown the beef all over. Add the onions and brown them. Cut the carrots and celery into large pieces and add them to the pan. Cook for another 2–3 minutes.

2 Meanwhile, add 1¾ cups hot stock to the beef. Bring to a boil, season and cover.

3 Cook in the oven for about 2 hours. Turn the brisket over and add more stock, if necessary. There should be enough liquid to come halfway up the meat and to make a thin but rich gravy. Continue cooking for about 1 hour.

4 Slice the meat and serve, surrounded by the vegetables. Garnish with flat leaf parsley.

Roasted Lamb with Zucchini

Racks of tender baby lamb chops, roasted pink on the inside, are a favorite choice for celebratory dinners.

INGREDIENTS

Serves 4

2 small racks lamb, each with 6 chops, or 3 racks lamb, each with 4 chops
4 tablespoons olive oil
juice of 1 pomegranate
1 tablespoon French mustard
4 sprigs fresh mint
4 zucchini, quartered lengthwise
½ cup light vegetable or chicken stock
2 tablespoons toasted pine nuts
salt and ground black pepper

1 Arrange the racks of lamb in a glass or ceramic dish. In a glass jar mix together 1 tablespoon olive oil, the pomegranate juice, mustard, salt and pepper. Add a few mint leaves and pour this marinade over the lamb. Chill for a couple of hours.

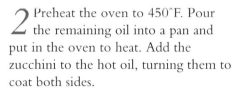

2 Preheat the oven to 450°F. Pour the remaining oil into a pan and put in the oven to heat. Add the zucchini to the hot oil, turning them to coat both sides.

3 Put the lamb in a roasting pan, with the fat side up. Roast the lamb and the zucchini for 20 minutes.

4 Transfer the racks of lamb to a serving dish and let them rest for 5 minutes, lightly covered with a sheet of foil. Pour the remaining marinade into the roasting pan and deglaze the pan with the vegetable or chicken stock. Heat and pour into a sauceboat.

5 Slice each rack of lamb into chops and arrange them on plates. Sprinkle the pine nuts over the zucchini. Serve the sauce separately and garnish the lamb with mint.

COOK'S TIP

To make pomegranate juice, halve the fruit and squeeze, like a lemon.

Slow-cooked Lamb with Barley

A perfect sabbath dish, which can be safely left and cooked for many hours.

INGREDIENTS

Serves 4–6
1–2 tablespoons oil
2 pounds shoulder of lamb, cubed
2 large onions
6 carrots or potatoes
²/₃ cup barley
3–5 cups boiling stock or water and
   1 kosher beef stock cube
chopped thyme, to garnish
salt and ground black pepper

1 Heat half the oil in a non-stick frying pan and sauté the cubes of lamb until brown all over. Transfer the meat to a large plate.

2 Cut the onions and carrots into small pieces (thinly slice the potatoes, if using) and sauté these in the remaining oil. Add the barley and seasoning, pour in half the stock and bring the liquid to a boil. Cook for about 5 minutes.

3 Pour the vegetables and barley into the bottom of a crockpot, cover with the lamb cubes and add enough stock to make a gravy. (See Cook's Tip.) Cover and cook for 6–9 hours or more. Check for seasoning, stir well and serve garnished with thyme.

COOK'S TIP

A crockpot is ideal for very gentle cooking as the gravy will not dry up. If you are using a conventional low oven, at 225°F, the liquid tends to evaporate, so use more liquid and check the pot occasionally.

VEGETABLES AND SIDE DISHES

Vegetables are never simply boiled or steamed, they are fried or roasted to accentuate their taste. Onions are essential for the sweet flavor they give almost any meat dish. Stuffed or broiled bell peppers, eggplants and zucchini are popular in Sephardic cooking, as is garlic.

As well as salads of mixed green leaves, there are rice salads with nuts and dried fruits, and cracked wheat, which is transformed into tabbouleh with fresh mint and parsley. Potato salad is a must.

Fresh, young vegetables like beets and green cucumbers make any table look attractive, but the original idea for large families was to stretch the main course with filling side dishes.

Roasted Pepper Salad

Mixed bell peppers should include green ones, but the orange, yellow and red are the sweetest. This colorful salad can be served either as an appetizer or as an attractive side dish to accompany cold meat dishes.

INGREDIENTS

Serves 6–10 as part of a buffet
6 bell peppers, in mixed colors
6–8 tablespoons olive oil
salt and ground black pepper

1 Preheat the oven to 375°F. Halve the peppers and remove all the seeds and membranes. Cut them into 1-inch strips.

2 Pour half of the oil into a roasting pan and put the pan into the oven for a few minutes to heat. Arrange the peppers in a single layer over the oil, turning them to make sure they are well-coated. Season well and drizzle over the remaining oil.

3 Roast for 20–30 minutes, turning them around once to ensure that those at the edges don't brown more than those in the center.

4 Turn the peppers out onto a large plate and let cool slightly. With a sharp knife, peel off the charred skin. Arrange the peeled peppers in groups of red, yellow and green on a decorative dish.

Tabbouleh

A salad that actually improves if it is made the day before. The bulgur, or cracked wheat, is uncooked and absorbs the moisture and flavor of the vegetables and dressing.

INGREDIENTS

Serves 4–6
1 cup bulgur
6-inch piece of cucumber
2 tomatoes
3–4 scallions
several sprigs fresh mint (about 4 tablespoons, chopped)
6 tablespoons finely chopped fresh parsley
5 tablespoons olive oil
2 tablespoons lemon juice
salt and ground black pepper

1 Cover the bulgur with water and leave to soak in a bowl for about 30 minutes. Drain through a fine strainer.

2 Peel and dice the cucumber. Peel the tomatoes by soaking for a minute in boiling water. Chop the flesh into small pieces, discarding the seeds. Slice the scallions.

3 Mix the drained bulgur with the vegetables and herbs. Whisk the oil with the lemon juice and seasoning and stir into the bulgur. Chill until required, but serve at room temperature.

COOK'S TIP

Tabbouleh can be served with lettuce leaves. Guests "wrap" the tabbouleh in the lettuce and eat it with their hands.

Pickled Cucumbers

Often served with salt beef, these gherkins or cucumbers are simple to prepare, but take a couple of days for the flavor to develop.

INGREDIENTS

Serves 6–8
6 small pickling cucumbers
5 tablespoons white wine vinegar
2 cups cold water
1 tablespoon salt
2 teaspoons sugar
10 black peppercorns
1 garlic clove
1 bunch fresh dill (optional)

1 You will need a large lidded jar or an oblong non-metallic container with a tightly fitting lid. Cut each cucumber lengthwise into six spears.

2 Mix together the wine vinegar, water, salt and sugar. Crush a few of the peppercorns and leave the rest whole. Add them to the liquid. Cut the garlic clove in half.

3 Arrange the cucumber spears in the jar or container, pour over the pickling liquid and add the garlic. Put in a few sprigs of dill, if using. Make sure they are completely submerged.

4 Leave the cucumbers, covered, in the fridge for at least two days. To serve, lift them out and discard the garlic, dill and peppercorns. Store any uneaten cucumbers in their pickling liquid in the fridge.

Potato Salads

Most people adore potato salad made with a creamy mayonnaise. These two versions are lighter and more summery. The first one should be served warm – the second can be prepared a day ahead and served cold.

INGREDIENTS

Serves 4
2 pounds new potatoes
1 teaspoon salt

Dressing for warm salad
2 tablespoons hazelnut or walnut oil
4 tablespoons sunflower oil
juice of 1 lemon
15 pistachio nuts
salt and ground black pepper
flat leaf parsley, to garnish

Dressing for cold salad
1 bunch parsley (about 6 tablespoons,
   chopped)
2 large scallions
5 tablespoons olive oil
2 teaspoons white wine vinegar
1 garlic clove, crushed
salt and ground black pepper

1 Scrub the new potatoes, cover with cold water and bring to a boil. Add the salt and cook for about 10–15 minutes, until tender. Drain well and set aside.

2 For the warm salad, mix together the hazelnut or walnut oil with the sunflower oil and lemon juice and season well.

3 Use a knife to crush the pistachio nuts coarsely.

4 When the potatoes have cooled slightly, pour over the dressing and sprinkle with the chopped nuts. Serve garnished with flat leaf parsley.

5 For the cold salad, cook the potatoes as previously, drain and set aside to cool. Meanwhile chop the parsley and the scallions finely.

6 Whisk together the oil, vinegar, garlic seasoning and herbs, and pour over the potatoes. Cover tightly and chill overnight. Allow to come to room temperature before serving.

Spiced Rice

Rice is served for everyday meals and feasts. Tender baby lamb was used in a celebrated dish called "King's Rice" but spices, nuts and dried fruit can be used to make plain rice very special.

INGREDIENTS

Serves 4–6
1 cup basmati rice
2 tablespoons oil
1-inch cinnamon stick
¼ teaspoon ground turmeric
¼ teaspoon tomato paste
1 tablespoon raisins
1 ounce toasted almonds
salt and ground black pepper

1 First cook simple boiled rice. Using a strainer, rinse the rice very well in cold running water until the water runs clear.

2 Add the rice to a saucepan of fast boiling water, add 1 teaspoon salt and boil for about 5–7 minutes or until the grains are tender. Drain and rinse with a little boiling water.

3 To make spiced rice, heat the oil in a large frying pan. Add the cinnamon stick and the turmeric and then the boiled rice. Stir well and heat thoroughly. Mix in the tomato paste and the raisins and taste for seasoning.

4 Remove the cinnamon stick and serve, sprinkled with almonds.

— COOK'S TIP —

Pouring water through the boiled rice removes the starch. To make the spiced rice you can boil the rice in advance and pour cold water through it and let it cool. Continue from Step 2, making sure the rice is quite hot before serving.

Bulgur Pilaf

Bulgur – or cracked wheat – is far easier to cook than rice. For every cup of grain you simply need two cups of liquid. Then you can add herbs, nuts or dried fruits to make the pilaf more interesting.

INGREDIENTS

Serves 8
2 onions
4 tablespoons oil
2 cups bulgur wheat
4 cups hot chicken or "chicken flavor" stock
2–3 sprigs fresh mint or flat leaf parsley
3–4 dried apricots, sliced
3 tablespoons pine nuts, toasted
salt and ground black pepper
sprig of mint, to garnish

1 Chop the onions finely. Heat the oil in a large frying pan and when it is hot toss in the onion. Stir over medium to high heat until the onion is slightly browned.

2 Wash the bulgur and drain. Add the bulgur to the sautéed onion and stir for a few minutes to coat the grains with the oil, adding a little more if necessary.

3 Add the stock. Bring to a boil, turn off the heat and cover.

4 Stand for 10 minutes. Meanwhile, chop the herbs. Check the seasoning and add the apricots.

5 To serve, spoon the hot bulgur into a large dish and sprinkle over the herbs and toasted pine nuts. Garnish with a sprig of mint.

Spicy Carrots

Adding spices to the carrots before leaving them to cool infuses them with flavor – an ideal dish to serve cold the next day (or up to a week later, if you keep it in the fridge).

INGREDIENTS

Serves 4
1 pound carrots
2 cups water
½ teaspoon salt
1 teaspoon cumin seeds
½–1 red chili (to taste)
1 large garlic clove, crushed
2 tablespoons olive oil
1 teaspoon paprika
juice of 1 lemon
flat leaf parsley, to garnish

1 Cut the carrots into slices about ¼-inch thick. Bring the water to a boil and add the salt and carrot slices. Simmer for about 8 minutes or until the carrots are just tender, without allowing them to get too soft. Drain the carrots, put them into a bowl and set aside until needed.

2 Grind or crush the cumin to a power. Remove the seeds from the chili and chop the chili finely. Take care when handling, as chilis can irritate the skin and eyes.

3 Gently heat the oil in a pan and toss in the garlic and the chili. Stir over medium heat for about a minute, without allowing the garlic to brown. Stir in the paprika and the lemon juice.

4 Pour the warm mixture over the carrots, tossing them well so they are coated with the spices. Spoon into a serving dish and garnish with a sprig of flat leaf parsley.

Potato Latkes

Latkes, or pancakes, should be piping hot and are sometimes served with hot salt beef or salami. Or serve as a delicious snack with apple sauce and sour cream.

INGREDIENTS

Serves 4
2 medium potatoes
1 onion
1 extra large egg, beaten
2 tablespoons matzo meal
oil, for frying
salt and ground black pepper

1 Grate the potatoes and the onion coarsely. Put them in a large colander but don't rinse them. Press them down, squeezing out the thick starchy liquid.

2 Immediately, stir the beaten egg into the drained potato and onion mixture. Add the matzo meal, stirring well to mix. Season with plenty of pepper and salt.

3 Pour some oil into a frying pan to a depth of about ½ inch. Heat the oil for a few minutes. (Test it by throwing in a small piece of bread, which should sizzle.) Take a spoonful of the latke mixture and lower carefully into the oil. Continue adding spoonfuls, not too close together, over the bottom of the pan.

4 Flatten the pancakes slightly with the back of a spoon and after a few minutes, when the latkes are golden brown on one side, carefully turn them over and continue frying until the other side is golden brown.

5 Drain the latkes on paper towels and serve immediately.

Eggplants with Garlic and Tomato Glaze

An unusual way of cooking eggplants, which tend to absorb large amounts of oil when fried. Roasting the slices in the oven makes them slightly crisp.

INGREDIENTS

Serves 4 as a side salad
2 eggplants, about 8 ounces each
2 garlic cloves
3 tablespoons tomato paste
6–8 tablespoons olive oil
½ teaspoon sugar
salt and ground black pepper
chopped flat leaf parsley, to garnish

> ——— COOK'S TIP ———
>
> If the slices are very thin they tend to burn easily, so check after 15 minutes and move them around in the pan.

1 Slice the eggplants about ¼ inch thick and spread them out on paper towels. Sprinkle with salt and let stand for about 30 minutes. This will remove any bitter taste from the eggplants.

2 Preheat the oven to 375°F. Crush the garlic cloves and stir in the tomato paste, 1 tablespoon oil and the seasoning. Pour about 4 tablespoons oil into a baking pan.

3 Rinse the eggplant slices in water, drain and dry them well. Arrange them on the oiled pan in a single layer. Spoon a little of the garlic-tomato mixture over each one. Drizzle over the remaining oil and bake the slices for about 30 minutes.

4 Carefully lift them off with a spatula and arrange them, slightly overlapping, in a circle on a flat dish. Garnish with chopped parsley.

Fresh Beets with Sour Cream

Freshly cooked summer beets have a brilliant color and taste. They can also be made into a cold soup, *Borscht,* by grating the cooked beets and adding it to the cooking liquid with lemon juice and sour cream.

INGREDIENTS

Serves 4
1 pound small uncooked beets
1¼ cups sour cream
salt and ground black pepper
dill sprigs, to garnish

1 Cut off the leaves about 1 inch from the top of the beets and remove the thin roots at the other end. Wash the beets very well, removing any dirt with a vegetable brush.

2 Cover the beets with water, season well, bring to a boil and simmer for about 30–40 minutes, or until they are soft. They are cooked when the skin peels off easily. Drain the beets, and when they have cooled slightly, use a knife to peel off the skin.

3 Spoon some of the sour cream onto individual plates, cut the beets into wedges and slide one of them over the sour cream to make a pretty pink swirl. Arrange the rest of the quarters around the edge and serve garnished with dill sprigs.

POULTRY

With its crisp skin and dark flesh, duck is an
extremely popular bird. Unless you can catch one,
you won't see pigeon or quail on the table because
kosher birds are never shot.
In Eastern Europe goose was a commonly eaten
bird and the rendered fat was used for frying.
Chicken fat, too, was used instead of butter to
flavor potatoes and the famous chopped liver.
In our more health-conscious age, chicken and
turkey are extremely popular, and for cooking,
most people use non-stick pans and a small
amount of olive or sunflower oil. It is largely a
matter of taste, so approximate quantities of oil are
often given in the recipes.

Cold Sliced Roast Chicken

Cooking the chestnut stuffing under the skin keeps the breast meat succulent and creates a striped effect when carved.

INGREDIENTS

Serves 6–8, or more as part of a buffet
2 onions, halved
2–3 tablespoons oil
1¼ cups fresh breadcrumbs
¾ cup unsweetened chestnut purée
5 pounds fresh, free-range chicken
salt and ground black pepper
lettuce leaves and potatoes, to serve
flat leaf parsley, to garnish

1 Chop one of the onions finely. Heat half of the oil in a small pan and sauté the onion until golden. Stir in ½ cup boiling water, take the pan off the heat and let stand for 5 minutes to absorb some of the liquid.

2 Mix together the breadcrumbs, onion and chestnut purée with any liquid in the pan. Season well. Set aside to cool completely.

3 Preheat the oven to 425°F. Wipe the chicken well with paper towels, inside and out, and carefully slide your hand under the skin on the breast to ease it away from the meat. Press the stuffing underneath the skin all over the breast.

4 Brush a roasting pan with the remaining oil and put in the chicken, breast side down, with the remaining onion halves. Roast for 1 hour, basting occasionally and pouring off any excess.

5 Turn the chicken over so that the breast is uppermost and continue to roast for another 15 minutes, covering the top with a strip of foil if it looks too brown.

6 When the chicken is cooked, let it cool before cutting downwards into slices. Serve with lettuce leaves and potatoes and garnish with flat leaf parsley.

Golden Chicken

One of those rare dishes that is better cooked in advance and reheated. The chicken (preferably an old boiling one and not a young roaster) cooks in its own rich gravy. Letting it cool helps in the removal of any fat and improves the flavor.

INGREDIENTS

Serves 5–6

1–2 tablespoons oil
5½ pounds free-range chicken
2 tablespoons all-purpose flour
½ teaspoon paprika
2½ cups boiling water
salt and ground black pepper
potatoes or rice and broccoli, to serve

1 Preheat the oven to 325°F. Heat the oil in a large flameproof casserole and sauté the chicken slowly on all sides until the skin is brown. A boiling fowl is fatter, so you should prick all over the skin with a fork on the back and legs to release the fat as the chicken cooks.

2 Put the chicken on a plate and sprinkle the flour into the remaining oil, adding a little more if necessary to make a paste. Add the paprika and seasoning and slowly pour in the boiling water, stirring all the time to make a thick sauce. When the sauce is simmering, replace the chicken, spoon some of the sauce over the top and cover tightly with a sheet of foil and then the lid.

3 Cook in the center of the oven for about 1 hour and then turn the chicken over. Continue cooking for about 2 hours or until the chicken is tender (a roaster will cook far more quickly than a boiler). Add a little extra boiling water if the sauce is drying up.

4 When the meat on the legs is soft, the chicken is done. Set aside to cool and pour the gravy into a bowl. When it is cold, chill in the fridge until the fat solidifies into a pale layer on the top. Remove with a spoon.

5 Bone the chicken and pour over the cold gravy. Reheat until the gravy is very hot and serve with boiled potatoes or rice and broccoli.

Noodles with Eggplants and Chicken Livers

Noodle dough used to be made into little meat-filled pockets called *kreplach* which were served in soup. This modern pasta recipe has an unusual sauce.

INGREDIENTS

Serves 4
For the sauce
2 large eggplants, about 12 ounces each
2 garlic cloves
1 large onion
6−8 tablespoons oil
1¼ pounds carton strained tomatoes
1 cup boiling water
salt and ground black pepper
chopped flat leaf parsley, to garnish

For the noodles
1½ pounds flat noodles
10 ounces chicken livers

1 Peel and dice the eggplants. Sprinkle with salt and drain on paper towels for 30 minutes. Rinse and squeeze dry. Crush the garlic and chop the onion.

2 Put half the oil in a frying pan and sauté the onion for about 1 minute. Add the garlic and cook until the onion starts to brown. Transfer to a plate and brown the eggplant in the remaining oil.

3 Spoon over the onion, add the strained tomatoes, boiling water and seasoning. Simmer for 30 minutes .

4 Preheat the broiler. Cook the noodles for 8 minutes. Meanwhile, broil the chicken livers on oiled foil for 3−4 minutes on each side. Cut into strips. Drain the noodles, spoon over the eggplant sauce and top with the chicken livers. Toss and serve, garnished with flat leaf parsley.

Chicken with Pimientos

Pimiento is the Spanish word for pepper.

INGREDIENTS

Serves 6
5 pounds roasting chicken
1 large onion
2 garlic cloves
3 ripe tomatoes, chopped
2 large red bell peppers
4−6 tablespoons olive oil
1 tablespoon sugar
salt and ground black pepper
flat leaf parsley, to garnish
6−8 pitted black olives and boiled
   rice, to serve

1 Preheat the oven to 375°F. Bone the chicken and cut into eight pieces. Slice the onion and crush the garlic. Peel and chop the tomatoes and seed and slice the peppers.

2 Heat half the oil in a large frying pan and sauté the onion, garlic and peppers for 3 minutes. Transfer to an ovenproof dish and then fry the chicken pieces and add to the dish.

3 Fry the tomatoes in the remaining oil for a few minutes. Add seasoning, sugar and 1 tablespoon water, then spoon over the chicken. Cook uncovered in the oven for about 1 hour. Cover if the chicken is getting too brown. Halfway through, pour the juices into a jug. Serve with black olives and boiled rice, and garnish with parsley. Pour the fat off the juices in the jug and pass round as extra gravy.

Chicken Pie with Mushrooms

The filling in this pie has an intense mushroom flavor, using chicken stock rather than the more usual milk and butter.

INGREDIENTS

Serves 4–6
For the pastry
5 ounces kosher margarine, chilled
2 cups all-purpose flour
1 egg yolk
4 tablespoons cold water

For the pie filling
2 pounds cooked roast or
   boiled chicken
3 tablespoons olive oil
10 ounces mixed dark mushrooms
   (Portobello, oyster or Crimini)
1½ tablespoons flour
1¼ cups chicken stock
1 tablespoon soy sauce
1 egg white
salt and ground black pepper

1 For the pastry, cut the margarine into small pieces and rub or cut it into the flour until it is like breadcrumbs. Mix the egg yolk with the cold water and stir it into the flour mixture. Form the dough into a ball, cover and chill for about 30 minutes.

2 Preheat the oven to 425°F. For the filling, cut the cooked chicken into pieces and put them in a greased pie plate about 7½ cup capacity.

3 Heat half the oil in a frying pan. Slice the mushrooms thickly and sauté them over high heat for about 3 minutes. Add the rest of the oil and stir in the flour. Season with pepper and slowly add the stock, stirring to make a thick sauce.

4 Stir in the soy sauce, taste for seasoning and pour the mushroom sauce over the chicken. Roll out the pastry and cut one piece slightly larger than the size of the pie plate. Also cut some long strips about ³/₄-inch wide. Place these round the rim of the pie plate, then lift the pastry onto the top, pressing it down on top of the strips. Trim the edges with a knife.

5 Lightly whisk the egg white and brush it over the pie. Bake in the oven for about 30–35 minutes.

> — COOK'S TIP —
>
> The pie can be made in advance up to Step 4 and chilled overnight or frozen. To cook after freezing, leave at room temperature for a few hours and cook as above.

Chicken Breasts with Burnt Almond Stuffing

Breadcrumbs are often used in stuffings, but this one is made from crunchy vegetables and matzo meal, so it is suitable for Passover.

INGREDIENTS

Serves 4

4 fat scallions
2 carrots
2 stalks celery
2 tablespoons oil
4 tablespoons flaked almonds
1¼ cups chicken stock or 1 kosher
　chicken stock cube and boiling water
6 tablespoons matzo meal
4 chicken breasts with skin
salt and ground black pepper
dill sprigs, to garnish
mixed salad, to serve

COOK'S TIP

Freshly made chicken stock is always better than a stock cube, but as this is a quick midweek dish, the short-cut can be used.

1 Preheat the oven to 375°F. Slice the onions and chop the carrots and celery stalks into small pieces. Heat the oil in a frying pan and sauté the almonds until they are light brown. Remove with a slotted spoon and then sauté the chopped vegetables over medium heat for a few minutes.

2 Add the seasoning, and pour in half of the stock. Cook over high heat until the liquid is slightly reduced and the vegetables are just moist. Mix in the matzo meal and the almonds.

3 Ease the skin off the chicken breasts on one side and press some of the stuffing underneath each one. Press the skin back over the stuffing and slash the skin to stop it curling up. Arrange the breasts in a roasting pan.

4 Roast the chicken breasts, skin side up, for about 20–30 minutes or until the meat is tender and white. The skin should be crisp and brown.

5 Keep the chicken warm while you make the gravy. Pour the remaining stock into the roasting pan and over medium heat stir in any chicken juices or bits of stuffing. Bring to a boil and then strain into a pitcher. Serve with a mixed salad and garnish with a dill sprig.

Turkey Breasts with Wine and Grapes

Chicken and meat are never cooked with cream, so a good stock and wine provide the flavor in this velvety sauce.

INGREDIENTS

Serves 3
1 pound turkey breast, thinly sliced
3 tablespoons flour
3–4 tablespoons oil
½ cup kosher white wine or sherry
½ cup chicken stock
5 ounces white grapes
salt and ground black pepper
flat leaf parsley, to garnish
new potatoes or boiled rice,
   to serve (optional)

1 Put the turkey slices between sheets of wax paper and flatten them with a rolling pin. Season the flour with salt and pepper and toss each turkey slice in it so that both sides are well coated.

2 Heat the oil in a large frying pan and sauté the turkey slices for about 3 minutes on each side. Pour in the wine or sherry and boil rapidly to reduce it slightly.

3 Stir in the chicken stock, lower the heat and cook for another few minutes. Halve and seed the grapes and stir into the sauce. Serve with potatoes or rice, if using. Garnish with parsley.

COOK'S TIP

For a dark sauce, you could use Crimini mushrooms. Sauté them in the oil before you cook the turkey in Step 2.

Apple-stuffed Duck

Stuffing the duck breasts with whole apples keeps the slices moist and gives an attractive appearance when served cold.

INGREDIENTS

Serves 4 as a hot dish, more when served cold as part of a buffet
1½ ounces raisins or sultanas
2 tablespoons kosher brandy
3 large onions
2 tablespoons oil
6 ounces fresh breadcrumbs
2 small apples, preferably McIntosh
2 large duck breasts, including the skin
salt and ground black pepper
mixed leaf salad, to serve

1 Soak the dried fruit in the brandy. Preheat the oven to 425°F.

2 Chop one onion finely and sauté it in the oil until golden. Season with salt and pepper and add ¼–½ cup water. Bring to a boil and then add breadcrumbs until the stuffing is moist but not sloppy.

3 Core and peel the apples. Drain the raisins and press them into the center of the apples. Flatten the duck breasts and spread out, skin side down.

4 Divide the stuffing between them and spread it over the meat. Place an apple at one end of each duck breast and carefully roll up to enclose the apples and stuffing. Secure with a length of cotton or fine string. Quarter the remaining onions. Prick the duck skin in several places to release the fat.

5 Arrange on a rack in a roasting pan with the onions underneath. Roast for about 35 minutes. Pour off the fat and roast at 325°F for about another 30–45 minutes.

6 To serve cold, set aside until cooled, chill, and then cut each breast into 5 or 6 thin slices. Arrange on a platter and bring to room temperature before serving. Serve with a salad.

DESSERTS

Our grandparents would probably have ended a meal with lemon tea or black coffee, some stewed fruit and a slice of sponge cake, called plava. *Cooks are more inventive today and have devised delicious dairy-free desserts, which are also light and more in line with current eating trends. The mounds of whipped cream that used to adorn trifles and gâteaux have been replaced by fresh-tasting fruit sauces and sorbets. Cheesecake, often considered to be American, was almost certainly brought to the New World from Hungary. Any dessert with cream is suitable to end a fish meal, but I have concentrated on pancakes, tarts and cakes where the emphasis is on fruit and berries. Lemon tea is still a good way to end a meal and for those who like a light fragrant drink, mint or jasmine tea are both refreshing.*

Hazelnut Sponge Cake

A dessert for Passover, that does not contain flour. The accompanying coulis is good after a meat meal, and the vanilla sauce containing milk is suitable after a vegetarian or a fish main course.

INGREDIENTS

For the hazelnut sponge
6 large eggs, separated
³/₄ cup superfine sugar
juice and grated rind of 1 lemon
³/₄ cup ground hazelnuts
1 ounce matzo meal
oil, for greasing

1 Preheat the oven to 350°F. Whisk the egg yolks with the sugar until the mixture is pale, thick and mousse-like. Add the juice and grated rind of the lemon.

2 Whisk the egg whites until stiff. Add a quarter of the whisked whites to the yolk mixture and then fold in the hazelnuts, the matzo meal and the remaining whites. Take care not to deflate the mixture.

3 Pour the mixture into a greased 10-inch cake pan and bake for 30–40 minutes. The center should be dry when tested with a cocktail stick or thin skewer.

4 When the cake is cool, take it out of the pan and store, covered, until ready for use. Serve it in wedges with Vanilla Sauce or Fruit Coulis.

Fruit Coulis and Vanilla Sauce

These two sauces make a delicious combination or they can be served separately.

INGREDIENTS

For the fruit coulis
1 cup blackberries or strawberries
2 tablespoons superfine sugar
1–2 tablespoons water

For the vanilla sauce
2 teaspoons potato starch
2 tablespoons vanilla sugar
3 egg yolks (or 2 small eggs)
1¼ cups milk

1 For the coulis, put the berries in a pan with the sugar and water. Cook over low heat just until the berries collapse.

2 Strain the fruit and juice through a nylon sieve into a pitcher.

3 For the vanilla sauce, mix the potato starch, sugar and egg yolks to a paste. Add the cold milk.

4 In a small pan over low heat bring the mixture slowly to a boil, stirring constantly. It will thicken after about 5 minutes. Take it off the heat, strain and let cool.

COOK'S TIP

Store a cut vanilla pod in a jar of sugar. The sugar will absorb the vanilla flavour.

Fruit Tree

A suitable pie for *Tu B'Shvat*, at the end of winter, when the almond trees blossom in Israel.

INGREDIENTS

Serves 4–6

For the pastry

5 ounces kosher margarine, chilled
2 cups all-purpose flour
1 egg, separated
4 tablespoons cold water

For the filling

1 pound cooking apples, or fresh apricots or plums
4–8 tablespoons sugar

1 To make the pastry, rub or cut the margarine into the flour until it is like breadcrumbs. Add the egg yolk and water, mix and form the dough into a ball. Cover and chill the dough for 30 minutes.

2 Preheat the oven to 400°F. Peel and core the apples or pit the summer fruit, if using. On a piece of paper, draw and cut out a tree shape about 12 inches high.

3 Roll out the pastry and put the tree outline on top. Cut round the first tree and then repeat, cutting the second one about ½ inch larger.

4 Lift the smaller shape onto a flat baking sheet. Cover with thinly-sliced apples, or pitted fruit. Sprinkle over the sugar to taste, reserving 1 tablespoon for the top.

5 Cover the pie with the other tree outline, pressing it down at the edges. Whisk the egg white lightly and brush it all over the pie. Roll out the pastry trimmings and cut out some apple or plum shapes. Press these onto the tree and brush again with egg white. Sprinkle over the remaining sugar and bake for about 30–35 minutes.

6 Slide a spatula carefully underneath the tree when it has cooled, and transfer it to a large platter.

Pear and Almond Flan with Chocolate Sauce

INGREDIENTS

Serves 4–6
For the flan
8 ounces kosher pastry
2 eggs, separated
¼ cup superfine sugar
½ cup ground almonds
2 large comice or Bartlet pears

For the sauce
4 ounces semisweet dark chocolate
1 tablespoon maple or golden syrup
2 tablespoons hot water

1 Roll out the pastry on a lightly floured surface, and use it to line a 8–10-inch flan pan. Preheat the oven to 400°F. Bake unfilled, by lining the pastry with wax paper and baking beans or a double thickness of foil, for the first 10 minutes of cooking.

2 Meanwhile, make the filling. Whisk the egg yolks with the sugar until pale and thick. Whisk the whites in a separate bowl. Fold the ground almonds into the yolk mixture and then fold in the whites.

3 Peel and slice the pears. Take the pastry shell out of the oven, and turn the temperature down to 350°F. Remove the foil or beans and arrange the pears on the bottom. Spoon the almond mixture over the top, making sure the fruit is completely covered. Bake in the oven for about 15 minutes. The top will be slightly colored and the almond mixture will have set.

4 Make the sauce just before serving, otherwise it gets hard. Melt the chocolate in a bowl, either over simmering water or in the microwave for about 2 minutes. Stir in the syrup and hot water and mix until smooth.

5 Serve the warm flan in portions, with a little of the chocolate sauce on the side.

Haroset

Though sweet, Haroset is not really a dessert. It forms part of the symbolic feast (*Seder* service) held on the eve of Passover. Variations on this recipe go back for at least 2,000 years. Haroset is a finely chopped mixture which represents the mortar used by the Jewish slaves to make bricks in Egypt.

INGREDIENTS

Makes enough to fill a 12 ounce jar
1 large cooking apple
1/2 cup almonds, blanched
   and skinned
2 teaspoons ground cinnamon
2 tablespoons kosher sweet red wine

1 Peel, quarter and chop the apple. Chop it finely with the blanched almonds. If you are using a food processor, make sure you don't process the mixture too finely, it should still be crunchy.

2 Stir in the cinnamon and sweet wine and spoon the mixture into a jar. The color and flavor develop after an hour or two.

3 Serve as part of the *Seder* service or as a topping for *matzah* or matzo crackers.

VARIATIONS

This recipe is Ashkenazi, but Sephardim use a variety of other ingredients. Most common are dates, figs, sesame seeds, walnuts and raisins.

Red Fruit Salad

Cut fruit usually deteriorates quickly but the juices from lightly cooked mixed berries make a brilliant red coating, so this salad can be made the day before. It is also one of the quickest ways of making fruit salad for a crowd.

INGREDIENTS

Serves 8
1 cup raspberries or blackberries
1/4 cup red currants or black currants
2–4 tablespoons sugar
8 ripe plums
8 ripe apricots
1 cup seedless grapes
1/2 cup strawberries

1 Mix the berries and currants with 2 tablespoons sugar. Pit the plums and apricots, cut them into pieces and put half of them into a pan with all of the berries.

2 Cook over very low heat with about 3 tablespoons water, or in a bowl with no water, in the microwave, until the fruit is just beginning to soften and the juices are starting to run.

3 Let cool slightly and then add the reserved plums and apricots, and the grapes. Taste for sweetness and add more sugar if the fruit is too tart. Let the fruit salad cool, then cover and chill – overnight if necessary.

4 Just before serving, transfer the fruit to a serving bowl. Slice the strawberries and arrange them over the fruit in the bowl.

Lemon Mousse

A mousse without cream but with the tangy taste of lemons.

Ingredients

Serves 8

1 tablespoon kosher gelatin
juice and grated zest of
  4 unwaxed lemons
6 large eggs, separated
scant cup superfine sugar

> —— Cook's Tip ——
>
> It is important to add hot gelatin to a hot mixture or cool gelatin to a cool one, otherwise it becomes stringy.

1 Sprinkle the gelatin into a cup or small bowl and add about ½ cup lemon juice. Stir and leave for a minute to swell. Stand the cup in a little simmering water in the base of a saucepan and stir until the gelatin melts. It will be almost clear and quite thin. Take the cup out of the pan.

2 Whisk the egg yolks with ¾ cup sugar until the mixture is thick and very pale. Spoon it into the top part of a double boiler (or a bowl set over a pan of simmering water). Add 1 tablespoon lemon zest and the remaining lemon juice. Stir the mixture constantly until it just begins to thicken.

3 After about 5 minutes the mixture should be thick and warm. Test the temperature with your finger as it should be as hot as the gelatin. Pour the gelatin into the lemon mixture and stir for a couple of minutes.

4 Take the pan (or bowl) off the hot water and cool it quickly. Leave until cool, but not too cold.

5 Whisk the egg whites and when they begin to stiffen, add the remaining 2 tablespoons sugar. Gently fold them into the lemon yolk mixture.

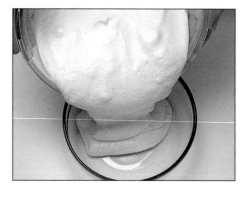

6 Pour the mousse into a glass bowl and decorate with lemon zest. Chill or freeze.

Pancakes with Fruit

Milk is usually a prominent ingredient in crêpes, but you can make thin pancakes with fresh orange juice instead.

INGREDIENTS

Makes about 12

1 cup all-purpose flour
pinch salt
1 beaten egg
⅔ cup fresh orange juice
⅔ cup iced water
oil, for frying
mint leaves, to decorate
fresh strawberries, sliced peaches and
   orange segments, to serve

1 Sift the flour and salt into a bowl. In another bowl, beat together the egg, orange juice and water.

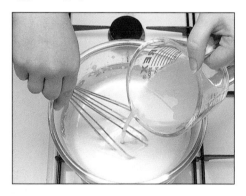

2 Make a well in the center of the flour and gradually beat in some of the egg mixture, stirring well to get rid of any lumps. Continue adding the liquid until you have a smooth batter. Chill for at least 30 minutes.

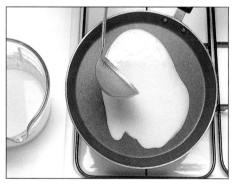

3 Pour a little oil into a small frying pan and turn on the heat. Then pour it back into a cup, leaving just a film on the bottom of the pan. When this is hot, pour in enough batter to thinly cover the base.

4 Slide a spatula around the edge and under the pancake and then turn it over. It should be golden. Cook the other side for about a minute, so that both sides are light brown.

5 Continue cooking the rest of the mixture until all the batter is used. Serve with fresh fruit.

COOK'S TIP

You can make the pancakes in advance, stack them between sheets of wax paper when they are cool, then store them in the fridge or freezer.

Cheesecake with Berries

Bought cheesecakes can be very sweet. This one is light and fresh.

INGREDIENTS

Serves 6–8
8 ounces graham crackers
3 ounces butter
5 eggs, separated
$2/3$ cup superfine sugar or
    vanilla sugar
2 cups cottage or ricotta cheese
$3/4$ cup sour cream
1 teaspoon vanilla extract (optional)
2 tablespoons self-rising flour, sifted
raspberries and blueberries, to serve
mint leaves, to decorate

1 Preheat the oven to 275°F. Crush the crackers finely and melt the butter in a pan over low heat. Mix the crumbs with the melted butter and press the mixture over the base and slightly up the sides of a loose-bottomed 8-inch cake pan.

2 Beat the egg yolks with the sugar and when they are pale and thick, add the cheese. Stir in the sour cream and vanilla extract, if using.

3 Whisk the egg whites until stiff and fold them in with the flour. Spoon the mixture into the prepared cake pan and bake for 45 minutes. Turn the oven off and leave for another hour without opening the oven door.

4 Take the cake out and let it cool completely in the pan. Remove and serve cool, but not chilled, with fresh raspberries and blueberries. Decorate with mint leaves.

Haman's Ears

These crisp lightly-sugared pastries are eaten on the Festival of Purim. Shaped like ears, the thin dough puffs up when fried. It is impossible to eat just one!

INGREDIENTS

Makes about 20 thin pastries
1 cup flour
$1/2$ teaspoon baking powder
1 egg
2 tablespoons water
few drops orange flower water
oil, for frying
confectioner's sugar, to decorate

1 Sift together the flour and baking powder and make a well in the center. Drop in the egg and add the water and orange flower water. Stir until the mixture forms a dough.

2 Roll out on a lightly-floured board, sprinkling the pin with flour to prevent sticking. When very thin, cut into 4-inch rounds. Re-roll the trimmings and use to cut more rounds.

3 Cut the circles in half, squeezing the centers slightly to make ear-shapes. Heat some oil in a deep pan and fry the ears, a few at a time, until they are golden brown. It only takes a few minutes.

4 Drain the pastries on paper towels and sprinkle with sifted confectioner's sugar. They will be quite dry and not at all oily. Serve cold with tea or coffee.

BREADS, CAKES AND PASTRIES

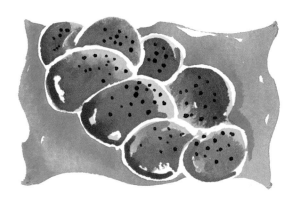

When coarse brown bread was considered everyday food, the special braided loaves always had to be made of fine white flour. So even though it is fashionable to eat dark nutty breads today, the sweet white challah has remained unchanged.

A family's origins are often reflected in the cakes and pastries served at their parties. Hand-made individual pastries like ma-amoul come from Egypt; apple pie or strudel from Austria. The most authentic of all Jewish cakes are those baked for Passover (with no flour or baking powder) and honey cake, served at New Year. Each slice carries with it hopes of a sweet year to come.

Challah

Braided *Challah* loaves are served at the sabbath meals.

INGREDIENTS

Makes 2 loaves
4 cups all-purpose flour
1½ teaspoons salt
2 teaspoons superfine sugar (optional)
2 teaspoons rapid-rise dried yeast
3 tablespoons oil
1 cup warm water
2 eggs
poppy seeds, to decorate

1 Sift together the flour, salt and sugar, if using, and sprinkle over the yeast. Mix the oil, half the water and 1 egg. The water must be warm, if too hot or too cold the bread won't rise. Add the remaining water to the flour and then the remaining liquid.

2 Mix together until a dough is formed then knead until smooth and elastic, using a little extra flour if it seems sticky.

3 Put the dough in a greased bowl, cover with a clean dish towel and leave in a warm place for at least 2 hours or until doubled in size. Punch down the dough by kneading it again and then divide it into two.

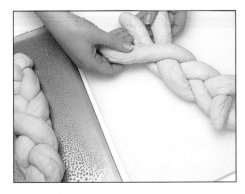

4 Cut each piece into three and roll them into long sausage shapes. Using three strands for each loaf, braid the dough and push the ends underneath. Let rise on an oiled baking sheet for about 30 minutes.

5 Preheat the oven to 425°F. Brush the loaves with egg, sprinkle with poppy seeds and bake for about 35 minutes. Cool on a wire rack.

Date Bread

Dates go back to biblical times. Dried fruits have natural sweeteners so this loaf needs no sugar added.

INGREDIENTS

Makes one loaf – about 16 slices
1⅓ cups dried dates, chopped
½ teaspoon baking soda
⅔ cup boiling water
1 egg
1 tablespoon butter, softened
⅔ cup self-rising flour
lightly salted butter, to serve

COOK'S TIP

Date bread keeps well for a few days wrapped in foil. To freeze, wrap in plastic wrap. Defrost for two hours before use.

1 Preheat the oven to 325°F. Put the dried dates in a bowl with the baking soda and boiling water. Let the dates soak for about 5 minutes.

2 Grease and line a 1 pound loaf pan with buttered wax paper so that it comes at least 1 inch above the pan.

3 Stir the egg, butter and flour into the date mixture and beat until smooth. The small pieces of date give the bread texture. Pour the mixture into the prepared pan.

4 Bake for about 1 hour in the center of the oven. Test for doneness with a strand of raw spaghetti or a thin skewer. When the bread is cool, take it out of the pan and remove the paper. Serve sliced and buttered.

Cinnamon Rolls

INGREDIENTS

Makes 24 small rolls
For the dough
1²/₃ cups all-purpose flour
½ teaspoon salt
2 tablespoons sugar
1 teaspoon rapid-rise dried yeast
3 tablespoons oil
1 egg
½ cup warm milk
/2 cup warm water

For the filling
2 tablespoons butter, softened
2 tablespoons dark brown sugar
½–1 teaspoon ground cinnamon
1 tablespoon raisins

1 Sift the flour, salt, and sugar and sprinkle over the yeast. Mix the oil, egg, milk and water and add to the flour. Mix to a dough, then knead until smooth. Let rise until doubled in size and then punch it down again.

2 Roll out the dough into a large rectangle and cut in half vertically. Spread over the soft butter, reserving 1 tablespoon for brushing. Mix the sugar and cinnamon and sprinkle over the top. Dot with the raisins.

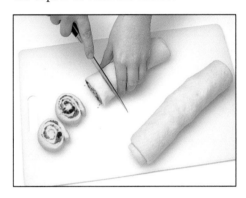

3 Roll each piece into a long Swiss roll shape, to enclose the filling. Cut into 1-inch slices, arrange flat on a greased baking sheet and brush with the remaining butter. Let rise again for about 30 minutes.

4 Preheat the oven to 400°F and bake the cinnamon rolls for about 20 minutes. Let cool on a wire rack. Serve fresh for breakfast or tea, with extra butter if liked.

Peach Kuchen

The joy of this cake is its all-in-one simplicity. It can be served straight from the oven, or cut into squares when cold.

INGREDIENTS

Serves 8

3 cups self-rising flour
1 cup superfine sugar
¾ cup unsalted butter, softened
2 eggs
½ cup milk
6 large peeled peaches, sliced or
   1 pound plums or cherries, pitted
½ cup brown sugar
½ teaspoon ground cinnamon
sour cream, to serve (optional)

1 Preheat the oven to 375°F. Lightly grease and line a 8 x 10 x 1 inch cake pan.

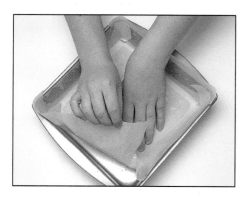

2 Put the flour, sugar, butter, eggs and milk into a large bowl and beat for a few minutes, until you have a smooth batter. Spoon it into the prepared cake pan.

3 Arrange the peaches, plums or cherries over the cake mixture. Mix the brown sugar and cinnamon and sprinkle over the fruit.

--- COOK'S TIP ---

To peel ripe peaches, cover with boiling water for 20 seconds. The skin will then slip off easily.

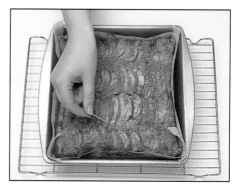

4 Bake for about 40 minutes, testing for doneness by inserting a toothpick in the center.

5 Serve the cake warm or cool with the sour cream, if you like.

Chocolate Brownies

The American versions of this recipe are usually rich in fat. The no-butter version still tastes dark and gooey, but is best eaten on the day it is made.

INGREDIENTS

Makes about 20
½ cup sunflower oil
5 ounces semisweet chocolate
2 eggs
1 cup self-rising flour
½ cup superfine sugar
1 teaspoon vanilla extract
1 cup halved pecan nuts

1 Preheat the oven to 400°F. Use a little of the oil to grease a 9-inch square shallow cake pan and line it with lightly oiled wax paper.

2 Melt the chocolate with the remaining oil in a bowl over simmering water (or in a microwave on high for about 2 minutes).

3 Beat the eggs lightly and add them to the chocolate, stirring vigorously. Beat in the flour, sugar and vanilla extract and pour the mixture into the pan. Arrange the pecans over the top.

4 Bake for about 10–15 minutes. If you like chewy brownies, take them out of the oven now. If you want a more cake-like finish, leave for 5 minutes. Cut into squares and cool before removing from the pan.

Honey Cake

The honey in this cake can be replaced by corn syrup but it needs natural brown sugar and ginger to give it the characteristic taste and color.

INGREDIENTS

6 tablespoons unsalted butter
6 tablespoons molasses or dark
  brown sugar
5 tablespoons honey or corn syrup
2 cups self-rising flour
¼ teaspoon baking soda
1 teaspoon ground ginger
⅔ cup milk
1 egg

1 Preheat the oven to 350°F. Grease and line a 1-pound loaf pan with a sheet of buttered wax paper.

2 Melt the butter, sugar and honey in a pan over very low heat, stirring constantly. Don't let the mixture boil.

3 Sift together the flour, baking soda and ginger and then stir in the milk and egg. Pour the honey mixture into the dry ingredients and beat well until smooth.

4 Pour into the prepared pan and bake in the oven for about 45 minutes. The cake will rise and should be dry in the middle when tested with a strand of raw spaghetti or a thin skewer.

5 Cool on a wire rack and then wrap the cake in foil. The flavor actually improves after a day.

Coconut Pyramids

Coconut cookies are sold in Israeli street markets during Passover.

INGREDIENTS

Makes about 15
1 cup unsweetened dried coconut
½ cup superfine sugar
2 egg whites
oil, for greasing

COOK'S TIP

To freeze cookies, arrange in a single layer on a tray. When hard, pack in bags or boxes. Defrost for one hour before use.

1 Preheat the oven to 375°F. Lightly grease a large baking sheet with a little oil.

2 Mix together the dried coconut and the sugar then lightly whisk the egg whites. Fold enough egg white into the coconut with a large spoon to make a fairly firm mixture. You may not need all the egg whites.

3 Form the mixture into pyramid shapes by taking a teaspoonful and rolling it first into a ball. Flatten the base and press the top into a point. Arrange the pyramids on the baking sheet, leaving a space between them.

4 Bake for 12–15 minutes on a low rack. The tips should begin to turn golden and the pyramids should be just firm, but still soft inside.

5 Slide a spatula carefully under the coconut pyramids to loosen them, and let cool before removing from the baking sheet.

Cinnamon Balls

Ground almonds or hazelnuts form the basis of most Passover cakes and biscuits. These balls should be soft inside, with a very strong cinnamon flavor. They harden with keeping, so it is a good idea to freeze some and use them only when required.

INGREDIENTS

Makes about 15

1½ cups ground almonds
⅓ cup superfine sugar
1 tablespoon ground cinnamon
2 egg whites
oil, for greasing
confectioner's sugar, for dredging

1 Preheat the oven to 350°F. Lightly grease a large baking sheet with a little oil.

2 Mix together the ground almonds, sugar and cinnamon. Whisk the egg whites until they begin to stiffen and fold enough into the almonds to make a fairly firm mixture.

3 Wet your hands with cold water and roll small spoonfuls of the mixture into balls. Place these at intervals on the baking sheet.

4 Bake for about 15 minutes in the center of the oven. They should be slightly soft inside – too much cooking will make them hard and tough.

5 Slide a spatula under the balls to release them from the baking sheet and let cool. Sift a few tablespoons of confectioner's sugar on to a plate and when the cinnamon balls are cold slide them on to the plate. Shake gently to completely cover the cinnamon balls in sugar and store in an airtight container or in the freezer.

Chocolate Apricots

Something to nibble with after-dinner coffee, these are simple and quick to make, but be certain to use the best quality chocolate rather than "chocolate flavor coating."

INGREDIENTS

Makes about 24
2 ounces semisweet chocolate
12 large dried apricots

COOK'S TIP

To melt this quantity of chocolate in the microwave, put it on a plate and cook on full power for about 1 minute.

1 Take a length of foil and line a baking sheet with it.

2 Melt the chocolate in a small bowl over simmering water.

3 Cut each apricot into 2–3 strips. Dip the long cut side of each strip into the melted chocolate and immediately place it on the foil. Put the tray of chocolate apricots in the freezer for about 30 minutes.

4 Slide them off the foil by pressing from underneath and store the apricots in a covered container in the fridge or the freezer. To defrost, arrange on a plate and leave for 30 minutes.

Baklava

Sweet syrup-soaked pastries are popular in Greece and the Middle East. This version is flavored with lemon and rosewater.

INGREDIENTS

Makes about 30
1 large cup shelled pistachio nuts
1 teaspoon superfine sugar
2 teaspoons rosewater
10 ounces filo pastry
1/4 cup oil

For the syrup
3/4 cup water
1 1/2 cups superfine sugar
juice of 1 lemon

1 Chop the pistachio nuts in a food processor. Don't grind them too fine. Stir in the sugar and rosewater.

2 Preheat the oven to 350°F. Cut the sheets of filo pastry in half. Brush a little oil on to the bottom and sides of a 10 inch square baking tin. Put in a sheet of pastry, brush with oil and cover with a second sheet. Use up half of the pastry this way.

3 Spread the nut mixture over the pastry and cover with a filo sheet. Repeat until oil and pastry is used up.

4 Using a sharp knife cut vertical lines 1 1/2 inches apart. Cut right through the pastry and nuts in diagonal lines across to form diamond shapes. Bake in the center of the oven for 15–20 minutes.

5 To make the syrup, put the water and sugar in a small pan and heat slowly. Stir once or twice and when it boils, add 2 tablespoons lemon juice. Boil the syrup for about 6 minutes. Stir in the remaining lemon juice and allow to cool and thicken slightly.

7 After 20 minutes, turn the oven temperature to 300°F and cook the baklava for another 20 minutes. Cool for about 10 minutes.

8 Pour the syrup over the baklava. Leave for several hours or overnight.

Ma-Amoul – Date-filled Pastries

From Gibraltar to Baghdad women would get together to make hundreds of these labor-intensive pastries. Making a small quantity is not so lengthy.

INGREDIENTS

Makes about 25
6 tablespoons margarine or butter, softened
1½ cups all-purpose flour
1 teaspoon rosewater
1 teaspoon orange flower water
3 tablespoons water

For the filling
²/₃ cup pitted dried dates
½ teaspoon orange flower water
4 teaspoons sifted confectioner's sugar, for sprinkling

1 To make the filling, chop the dates finely. Add ¼ cup boiling water and the orange flower water to the dates. Beat the mixture vigorously then set aside to cool.

2 To make the pastries, rub or cut the margarine or butter into the flour. Add the flower waters and the water and mix to a firm dough.

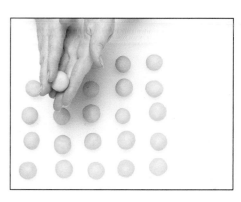

3 Shape the dough into about 25 small balls.

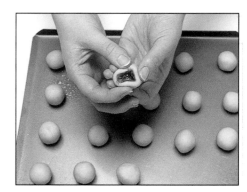

4 Preheat the oven to 350°F. Press your finger into each ball to make a small container, pressing the sides round and round to make the walls thinner. Put about ¼ teaspoon of the date mixture into each one and seal by pressing the pastry together.

5 Arrange the date pastries, seam side down, on a lightly greased baking sheet and prick each one with a fork. Bake for 15–20 minutes and let cool.

6 Put the cooled pastries on a plate and sprinkle over the confectioner's sugar. Shake lightly to cover. These pastries freeze well.

--- COOK'S TIP ---

The secret of good *ma-amoul* is to get as much date filling into the pastry as possible, but you must make sure to seal the opening well. The traditional way to decorate them was to make a pattern using tweezers but it is quicker to use a fork.

Flaked Almond Cookies

It is always useful to have a jar of crisp homemade cookies to offer around to friends.

INGREDIENTS

Makes about 30

³/₄ cup butter or
kosher margarine
2 cups self-rising flour, plus extra
for dusting
³/₄ cup superfine sugar
½ teaspoon ground cinnamon
1 egg, separated
2 tablespoons cold water
½ cup flaked almonds

1 Preheat the oven to 350°F. Rub the butter or kosher margarine into the flour. Reserve 1 tablespoon of the sugar and mix the rest with the cinnamon. Stir into the flour and then add the egg yolk and cold water and mix to a firm paste.

2 Roll the dough out on a lightly floured board and, when ½ inch thick, sprinkle over the almonds. Continue rolling, pressing the almonds into the dough so that it is about ¼-inch thick.

3 Using a fluted round cutter, cut the dough into rounds. Use a spatula to lift them onto an ungreased baking sheet. You can re-form the dough and cut more rounds to use it all up. Whisk the white of egg lightly and brush it over the cookies and sprinkle over the remaining sugar.

4 Bake in the center of the oven for about 10–15 minutes or until golden. To remove, slide a spatula under the cookies, which will still seem a bit soft, but they harden as they cool. Leave on a wire rack until completely cold. Store the almond cookies in an airtight container.

Index